AMERICA'S STORY

TEACHER'S GUIDE
THE COMPLETE EDITION ★ BOOK ONE ★ BOOK TWO

Harcourt Achieve

Rigby • Saxon • Steck-Vaughn

www.HarcourtAchieve.com
1.800.531.5015

Staff Credits

Executive Editor: Tina Posner
Supervising Editor: Donna Townsend
Editor: Linda Doehne

Design Staff: Stephanie Arsenault,
Donna Cunningham, Joan Cunningham,
Deborah Diver, John-Paxton Gremillion,
Scott Huber, Heather Jernt, Alan Klemp,
Joyce Spicer

ISBN 0-7398-9715-2

1 2 3 4 5 6 7 8 9 10 054 12 11 10 09 08 07 06 05

Curr
973
H25am
r2

The history of the United States is colorful and exciting. Yet, because many students throughout the nation have difficulty reading, they are unable to experience the adventure of American history. The high reading levels found in basal history textbooks prevent these readers from learning their nation's story. They are frequently discouraged and bored. There has been a lack of stimulating educational material on a low reading level. *America's Story* tries to address these problems.

STUDENT EDITION

America's Story is available in a two-volume, softcover edition (Bk 1, Units 1–4, and Bk 2, Units 1–5) and a complete, hardcover edition (CE, Units 1–9). Both editions present the history of the United States, from the cultural heritage of Native Americans to modern American achievements in world leadership and technology.

The cover of *America's Story* can help teachers introduce this subject area as a study of dramatic events, determined personalities, and lofty ideals. The American spirit of exploration, discovery, and invention is captured in the photos. Using pictures rather than words, the message conveyed is that history is a story of continual change encompassing the past, present, and future.

Special features have been incorporated into *America's Story* to make the material easier for students with learning difficulties. *America's Story* is written on a second- to third-grade reading level. Colorful maps, photographs, and illustrations have been carefully chosen to enhance the content. New vocabulary words are introduced at the beginning of each chapter under the heading **New Words**. They are presented in bold print when they first appear in the text. These vocabulary words are also defined in the glossary. Most vocabulary words are reviewed and reused throughout *America's Story*. The number of new vocabulary words in a chapter is carefully limited. Sentences in the text are simply and carefully structured, and idioms are kept at a minimum.

Other features in *America's Story* help students comprehend the material. The names of unfamiliar people and places that appear in the text are introduced at the beginning of each chapter under the heading **People and Places**. Unit openers provide background information and arouse interest in the material. Pre-reading questions help set a purpose for reading. Unit reviews help students recall significant events introduced in the unit.

There are two special features in each unit—**Using Primary Sources** and **Using Geography Themes**. More information about these features can be found on pages 9 and 10 of this guide.

Activities designed to ensure comprehension, improve skills, and broaden understanding follow each chapter:

- **Read and Remember** activities enable students to review their knowledge of American history and improve their reading comprehension and recall skills.
- **Think and Apply** and **Using Graphic Organizers** activities are designed to develop students' critical thinking skills and to show students how to organize information visually for easier recall. Recognizing main ideas, categorizing information, differentiating between fact and opinion, sequencing events, recognizing point of view, recognizing cause and effect, and drawing conclusions are some of the skills that are presented in *America's Story*. Students are taught each skill and then given ample opportunities for practice.
- **Skill Builders** develop the social studies skills students need to work with maps, time lines, charts, diagrams, tables, and graphs. Each skill is reinforced throughout the book. The skill lessons build upon and reinforce factual information covered in the chapters.
- **Journal Writing** allows students to respond to, and thereby assimilate, the content through written self-expression. A wide range of suggested activities gives students the opportunity to practice their writing skills, while demonstrating content knowledge.

America's Story includes the following additional features to help students develop reference skills.

- **Maps** are located at the back of the pupil edition for easy reference. These include a physical map of the United States, a political map of the United States, as well as a physical map of the world and a political map of the world.
- **The Fifty States** provides information on each state including its flag, capital city, population, land area, symbols, and date of statehood.
- **Territories and Possessions of the United States** provides information on the District of Columbia, Puerto Rico, and other outlying areas of the United States.
- **The Presidents of the United States** provides a portrait of each President and the years in office.
- **Glossary** defines the new vocabulary terms that appear in the pupil edition. Page numbers locate the first use of the term.
- **Index** gives an alphabetical list of names, places, and subjects that are discussed in the text.

Two major documents are also included in the text.

- **The Declaration of Independence** is provided on pages 322–326 in its entirety with an annotated version for students' study and reference.
- **The Constitution of the United States** is reproduced in full on pages 327–354 with an annotated version for students' study and reference.

TEACHER'S GUIDE

This Teacher's Guide has been designed to enhance the activities and learning opportunities contained in *America's Story*. It offers teaching strategies for all units and chapters, as well as blackline masters for review and assessment. Answer keys for all student edition activities and blackline masters are also provided. The following descriptions provide more detail.

The **Scope and Sequence** chart identifies in which units and chapters critical thinking skills, social studies skills, primary sources, and the five geography themes are introduced or reinforced. The chart also shows which of the social studies thematic strands are emphasized in each unit and chapter. The strands were developed by a task force of the National Council for the Social Studies.

Primary sources and geography themes are two features of *America's Story*. These features are explained on pages 9–10 of this guide. The **Primary Source Information for Teachers** page gives information for defining and analyzing primary sources. The **Five Themes of Geography** page discusses each of the five themes of geography.

Unit Teaching Strategies contain the following:

- **Summary** states the main ideas of the unit.
- **Major Concepts** list important concepts in the unit.
- **Pre-Reading Activities** offer a variety of activities to develop concepts and background information before reading the unit.
- **Post-Reading Discussion Points** offer topics that students can discuss together as a class or in small groups to reinforce comprehension and recall.
- **Follow-Up Activities** offer creative activities to review and extend the content of the unit.
- **Review Activities** are blackline masters in the Teacher's Guide that cover key concepts, events, and facts. There are reviews for every unit.
- **Assessment** provides blackline master tests for each unit. These tests are designed to encourage student success. There are tests for every unit.
- **Answer Key** provides the answers to all unit review activities and assessment activities found in the student edition and in the Teacher's Guide.

Chapter Teaching Strategies contain the following:

- **Summary** provides a brief overview of the chapter.
- **Objective** sets learning objectives for students.
- **Pre-Reading Activities** set the stage for successful reading and thorough comprehension.
- **Vocabulary Activities** offer creative opportunities for vocabulary building.
- **Review Words** are listed for teacher reference. They are vocabulary words from previous chapters that students will encounter in the new chapter.

- **Post-Reading Discussion Points** lead students to think critically about the chapter's content.
- **Primary Source Quote** provides background information about the primary source quote in the chapter.
- **ELL Activities** are designed to help students with limited English proficiency to learn the material in the chapter. The activity might also provide guided practice of essential vocabulary and concepts that are necessary background knowledge for understanding the material in the chapter.
- **Follow-Up Activities** offer kinesthetic, multi-sensory opportunities for concept assimilation.
- **Chapter Online Resources** provide more information about the topics in each unit at *www.HarcourtAchieve.com/AchievementZone*. Click on *America's Story*.
- **Answer Key** provides the answers to all chapter activities in the student edition.

Blackline Masters are provided for teacher use. These blacklines may be duplicated as needed:

- **Unit Reviews** cover key concepts and facts of the unit. One two-page review is included for each unit.
- **Unit Tests** cover key concepts and facts of the unit. One two-page test is included for each unit.
- **Time Line Reviews** focus on the significant historical events covered in several units and serve as a review for the final test. One time line review is provided for Bk 1 and CE, Units 1–4. One time line review is provided for Bk 2, Units 1–5; CE, Units 5–9.
- **Final Tests** are designed to assess student learning after several units of material. One two-page final test is provided for Bk 1 and CE, Units 1–4. One two-page final test is provided for Bk 2, Units 1–5; CE, Units 5–9.

Additional Blackline Masters are provided to enhance teaching opportunities. These blacklines may be reproduced as needed:

- **Pre-Reading Guide** helps the students establish a purpose prior to reading the text.
- **Graphic Organizers** help students organize the main ideas of the units and chapters. Suggestions for using the graphic organizers are included in the Teaching Strategies.
- **Geography Themes** can be tailored to a variety of subjects to help reinforce the five geography themes. Suggestions for using the geography theme blackline masters are included in the Teaching Strategies.
- **Writing Process Study Guide** provides a checklist to assist students in improving their writing.
- **Research on the Web Study Guide** guides students through researching on the Internet.
- **Maps** of the United States and the world allow students to build map skills. Suggestions for using these maps are included in the Teaching Strategies.

GENERAL TEACHING SUGGESTIONS

Teachers are encouraged to use the following suggestions where appropriate to their classroom situations and their students' needs.

1. Begin each unit by having students read and study the unit opener. Then refer to the **Unit Teaching Strategies** for introductory and follow-up activities.

2. Begin each chapter with the **Pre-Reading Activities** found in the **Chapter Teaching Strategies**.

3. Introduce the new vocabulary before students read the chapter. Suggestions for introducing new vocabulary are found in the **Chapter Teaching Strategies**. Help students pronounce the names listed in **People and Places**. Use a map to help students locate each place listed in **People and Places.**

4. Assist students as they read the chapter text. You may wish to have students read the text aloud. Point out how the illustrations, photographs, and maps enhance the text.

5. Discuss the questions provided in the **Chapter Teaching Strategies**. These questions serve as guidelines for understanding the text.

6. Students should complete the **Read and Remember** activities independently when possible. It may be helpful to go over the directions for each exercise with the class to be certain each student understands the procedure. When students cannot recall the answers from memory, encourage them to find the answers in the text. Reinforce skimming skills as needed.

7. Present new **Think and Apply, Using Graphic Organizers** and **Skill Builder** activities to the class in brief group lessons.

8. The development of writing skills in social studies is one of the goals of *America's Story*. Students should keep social studies notebooks for their writing activities. Discuss each journal writing activity with the class before students begin to write. Encourage students to use the **Writing Process Study Guide** on page 121 of this guide.

9. Make connections between past history and present events. For example, compare the exploration of America with the exploration of space. Urge students to record these connections in their journals.

10. Encourage additional independent student reading in social studies.

11. Use the **Graphic Organizer** blackline masters as suggested in the Teacher's Guide.

12. Encourage students to learn about current events through TV reports, newspapers, and the Internet.

13. Use the review tests and final tests included as blackline masters.

GRAPHIC ORGANIZERS

Graphic Organizers help students improve comprehension, critical thinking, and writing skills. They give learning a visual component and assist students in organizing information. Seven types of graphic organizers are included as blackline masters in this Teacher's Guide:

◆ **Concept Web** helps students develop the main idea and supporting facts, show a cause that has multiple effects, make word associations for vocabulary development, and write paragraphs based on the content of the concept web.

◆ **Sequencing** shows the order in which major events occurred. Have students use completed sequencing charts to write summaries of the events in a chapter.

◆ **Cause and Effect** helps students show how one cause is linked to two events or how two causes may result in one event.

◆ **Feature Chart** helps students categorize information, apply vocabulary, draw conclusions, and decide which facts are associated with a topic.

◆ **Event Description** helps students identify the important people, places, dates, causes, and effects of major historic events.

◆ **Main Idea and Supporting Details** helps students distinguish between a main idea and supporting details.

One or more of these graphic organizers can be used with every chapter in *America's Story*. Suggestions for use of these graphic organizers are included in the Teaching Strategies.

SCOPE & SEQUENCE

♦ = Student Edition
■ = Teacher's Guide
Bk 1/Bk 2 = Two-volume Edition
CE = Complete Edition

Unit	Chapter	Fact or Opinion	Main Idea	Cause and Effect	Drawing Conclusions	Point of View	Sequencing	Categories	Maps	Time Lines	Charts, Diagrams, and Tables	Graphs	Letters, Diaries, Artifacts, Quotations	Place	Location	Movement	Human/Environment Interaction	Region
Bk 1, Unit 1 / CE, Unit 1	Bk 1 and CE, Ch 1	♦							♦■				♦					
	Bk 1 and CE, Ch 2		♦						♦■				♦					
	Bk 1 and CE, Ch 3							♦	♦■				♦	♦■				
	Bk 1 and CE, Ch 4			♦■							♦							
	Bk 1 and CE, Ch 5						♦		♦		■		♦■					
	Bk 1 and CE, Ch 6	♦					■		♦■		■		♦	■				
Bk 1, Unit 2 / CE, Unit 2	Bk 1 and CE, Ch 7			■		♦				♦	■		♦					
	Bk 1 and CE, Ch 8				♦		■						♦■					
	Bk 1 and CE, Ch 9			♦								♦	♦					
	Bk 1 and CE, Ch 10						♦		♦■	■			♦		♦■			
	Bk 1 and CE, Ch 11		♦								♦■							
Bk 1, Unit 3 / CE, Unit 3	Bk 1 and CE, Ch 12						■	♦	♦■				♦	■				
	Bk 1 and CE, Ch 13			■	♦		♦CE				■		♦■					
	Bk 1 and CE, Ch 14			♦								♦						
	Bk 1 and CE, Ch 15	♦							♦				♦				♦■	
	Bk 1 and CE, Ch 16		♦	■							♦		♦					
Bk 1, Unit 4 / CE, Unit 4	Bk 1 and CE, Ch 17					♦	■		■				♦■					
	Bk 1 and CE, Ch 18			♦					♦■				♦			■		
	Bk 1 and CE, Ch 19							♦	♦■				♦			■	♦■	
	Bk 1 and CE, Ch 20	♦							♦■			♦						♦■
	Bk 1 and CE, Ch 21				♦CE		♦		■		♦		♦					■
Bk 2, Unit 1 / CE, Unit 5	Bk 2, Ch 1; CE, Ch 22		♦						■	■			♦■					
	Bk 2, Ch 2; CE, Ch 23			♦■					♦■	♦			♦					♦■
	Bk 2, Ch 3; CE, Ch 24	♦					♦CE ■		♦■				♦					■
	Bk 2, Ch 4; CE, Ch 25						♦				♦■		♦					
Bk 2, Unit 2 / CE, Unit 6	Bk 2, Ch 5; CE, Ch 26							♦	♦■			♦	♦	♦■				
	Bk 2, Ch 6; CE, Ch 27			♦					♦■		■		♦					■
	Bk 2, Ch 7; CE, Ch 28				♦							♦	♦					
	Bk 2, Ch 8; CE, Ch 29	♦		■									♦■					
	Bk 2, Ch 9; CE, Ch 30						■	♦				♦	♦					
Bk 2, Unit 3 / CE, Unit 7	Bk 2, Ch 10; CE, Ch 31		♦						♦■				♦					
	Bk 2, Ch 11; CE, Ch 32	♦							♦■	♦			♦			♦■		
	Bk 2, Ch 12; CE, Ch 33			♦■					♦				♦					
	Bk 2, Ch 13; CE, Ch 34					♦			■		♦		♦■	■				
	Bk 2, Ch 14; CE, Ch 35				♦				♦■				♦					
Bk 2, Unit 4 / CE, Unit 8	Bk 2, Ch 15; CE, Ch 36			■		♦			♦■				♦	■		■		
	Bk 2, Ch 16; CE, Ch 37	♦										♦						
	Bk 2, Ch 17; CE, Ch 38		♦										♦■					
	Bk 2, Ch 18; CE, Ch 39						■	♦	♦■			♦	♦		♦■			
	Bk 2, Ch 19; CE, Ch 40						♦		♦				♦					
	Bk 2, Ch 20; CE, Ch 41			♦					■			♦	♦					■
Bk 2, Unit 5 / CE, Unit 9	Bk 2, Ch 21; CE, Ch 42		♦						♦		■			■			♦■	
	Bk 2, Ch 22; CE, Ch 43		♦						■			♦			■			
	Bk 2, Ch 23; CE, Ch 44							♦					♦■				■	
	Bk 2, Ch 24; CE, Ch 45						♦ ■		♦ ■				♦	■				
	Bk 2, Ch 25; CE, Ch 46					■		♦					♦■					

7

◆ = Student Edition
■ = Teacher's Guide
Bk 1/Bk 2 = Two-volume Edition
CE = Complete Edition

	Culture	Time, Continuity, and Change	People, Places, and Environments	Individual Development and Identity	Individuals, Groups, and Institutions	Government	Economics	Science, Technology, and Society	Global Connections	Democratic Values
Bk 1, Unit 1 / CE, Unit 1										
Bk 1 and CE, Ch 1	◆	◆	◆■		◆					
Bk 1 and CE, Ch 2	◆		◆■				◆		◆■	
Bk 1 and CE, Ch 3	◆■	◆	◆	■	◆■		◆		◆■	
Bk 1 and CE, Ch 4	◆	◆	◆■		◆■	◆	◆		◆	◆
Bk 1 and CE, Ch 5	◆	◆	◆■	◆	◆■	◆	◆		◆	
Bk 1 and CE, Ch 6	◆■	◆	◆■			◆	◆	◆	◆	
Bk 1, Unit 2 / CE, Unit 2										
Bk 1 and CE, Ch 7		◆	◆		◆■	◆■			◆	■
Bk 1 and CE, Ch 8		◆		◆	◆■	◆■			◆	◆■
Bk 1 and CE, Ch 9		◆		◆■	◆■	◆■		◆■	◆	◆■
Bk 1 and CE, Ch 10				◆■	◆■	◆■	◆■			◆
Bk 1 and CE, Ch 11	■	◆	◆	◆■		◆■				◆■
Bk 1, Unit 3 / CE, Unit 3										
Bk 1 and CE, Ch 12	◆	◆	◆■	◆■	◆■	◆			◆	
Bk 1 and CE, Ch 13		◆■	◆■	◆■		◆■			◆	
Bk 1 and CE, Ch 14	◆■	◆■	◆■	◆■		◆	◆■	◆■	◆	
Bk 1 and CE, Ch 15	◆■	◆	◆■	◆■	◆■	◆■				◆■
Bk 1 and CE, Ch 16	◆■	◆	◆■	◆■	◆■	◆				◆■
Bk 1, Unit 4 / CE, Unit 4										
Bk 1 and CE, Ch 17		◆■	◆	◆■	◆■	◆■			◆	
Bk 1 and CE, Ch 18	◆	◆	◆■	◆■	◆■	◆■			◆	◆
Bk 1 and CE, Ch 19	◆	◆■	◆■	◆	◆		◆			
Bk 1 and CE, Ch 20	◆	◆■	◆■	◆	◆■	◆	◆■			
Bk 1 and CE, Ch 21	◆	◆■	◆■	◆	◆■	◆				
Bk 2, Unit 1 / CE, Unit 5										
Bk 2, Ch 1; CE, Ch 22	◆■	◆■	◆■	■	◆■	◆■		◆	◆	◆■
Bk 2, Ch 2; CE, Ch 23	◆■	◆■	◆■		◆■	◆	◆	◆■	◆	
Bk 2, Ch 3; CE, Ch 24	◆■	◆	◆	◆	◆■	◆■	◆		◆■	
Bk 2, Ch 4; CE, Ch 25	◆	◆■	◆■	◆■	◆■			◆■	◆■	
Bk 2, Unit 2 / CE, Unit 6										
Bk 2, Ch 5; CE, Ch 26	◆■	◆■	◆■	◆■	◆■		◆	◆■	◆	
Bk 2, Ch 6; CE, Ch 27		◆■			◆■	◆■	◆■			◆■
Bk 2, Ch 7; CE, Ch 28	◆■	◆■	◆■	◆■	◆■		◆■	◆■		◆
Bk 2, Ch 8; CE, Ch 29	◆■	◆■	◆■	◆■	◆■			◆■		◆■
Bk 2, Ch 9; CE, Ch 30	◆	◆■	◆	◆■	◆■	◆	◆■	◆		◆
Bk 2, Unit 3 / CE, Unit 7										
Bk 2, Ch 10; CE, Ch 31		◆■	◆	◆■	◆■	◆■		◆■	◆■	◆■
Bk 2, Ch 11; CE, Ch 32	◆■	◆■	◆■			◆■	◆■	◆	◆■	◆
Bk 2, Ch 12; CE, Ch 33	◆■	◆■	◆■			◆■	◆	◆■		◆
Bk 2, Ch 13; CE, Ch 34	◆	◆■	◆			◆■	◆■		◆	◆■
Bk 2, Ch 14; CE, Ch 35	◆	◆■	◆			◆	◆■		◆■	◆■
Bk 2, Unit 4 / CE, Unit 8										
Bk 2, Ch 15; CE, Ch 36	◆■	◆	◆■	◆■	◆	◆■			◆■	◆■
Bk 2, Ch 16; CE, Ch 37	◆■	◆	◆	◆■	◆■	◆	◆	◆■		◆■
Bk 2, Ch 17; CE, Ch 38	◆■	◆■	◆	◆■	◆■	◆■	◆■	■	■	◆■
Bk 2, Ch 18; CE, Ch 39	◆	◆	◆■		◆■	◆		◆■	◆■	
Bk 2, Ch 19; CE, Ch 40	◆■	◆	◆■	◆■	◆■	◆■			◆■	◆■
Bk 2, Ch 20; CE, Ch 41	◆■	◆	◆		◆■	◆■			◆■	◆■
Bk 2, Unit 5 / CE, Unit 9										
Bk 2, Ch 21; CE, Ch 42	◆■	◆■	◆■			◆■	◆■		◆■	◆■
Bk 2, Ch 22; CE, Ch 43	◆■	◆■	◆	◆	◆	◆■	◆		◆■	
Bk 2, Ch 23; CE, Ch 44	◆■	◆■	◆			◆■		◆■	◆■	
Bk 2, Ch 24; CE, Ch 45	◆	◆			◆	◆			◆	◆
Bk 2, Ch 25; CE, Ch 46	◆■	◆	◆	◆	◆	◆■	◆	◆	◆	◆■

DEFINING PRIMARY SOURCES

When studying a certain time period or event in the past, historians often use **primary sources**. A primary source is the original source of information from the time period being studied. It is information produced during or soon after the event, usually by someone who participated in or observed the event. There are many types of primary sources including oral histories, photographs, drawings, paintings, artifacts, first-person accounts, poems, songs, newspapers, and quotations. These first-hand accounts of history help students become more involved in their study of the era.

It is important to know the difference between a primary source and a **secondary source**. A secondary source is an artifact produced or an account written sometime after the event, usually by someone who was not an actual participant in the event. Secondary sources may be based on primary sources or on other secondary sources. An encyclopedia, a biography, and a textbook are all examples of secondary sources.

ANALYZING PRIMARY SOURCES

Primary sources provide a variety of perspectives on history. Primary sources can convey a strong sense of an event or historical period. But if the author/producer is personally involved in the event, the account may be biased or false. It is helpful to know the point of view of the author/producer of the primary source. Primary sources based on eyewitness accounts sometimes tell incomplete stories. Primary sources written or produced long after the event occurred are less likely to be reliable or accurate. As time passes, people's memories are less reliable, and forgotten details are sometimes filled with events that never took place. As a result, it is important to analyze primary sources to determine their reliability and accuracy. Use the following tips for analyzing a primary source.

A. **Identify the nature of the primary source.** What type of primary source is it? What is the subject of the primary source? Who wrote or produced it? When was it written or produced? How long after the event occurred was the primary source written/produced? Where did the author/producer get his or her information about the subject?

B. **Analyze the reliability of the primary source.** Does the author/producer have a certain bias or point of view toward the subject of the primary source? If so, what is the bias or point of view? How might this bias or point of view affect the reliability of the primary source? Is more than one point of view about the subject presented in the primary source? Is the account convincing? How does the author/producer know about the subject? What is the author/producer's background?

C. **Determine the accuracy of the primary source.** Can you find other primary or secondary sources that have the same point of view or draw the same conclusions as the author/producer of this primary source? Do the author's emotions or opinions influence the primary source? Why did the author/producer write or produce the primary source? Who is the author/producer's audience? Can you find information in dictionaries, encyclopedias, and maps to check the validity of the primary source?

TYPES OF PRIMARY SOURCES

- ◆ **Oral Histories** are myths, legends, memories, interviews, customs, and traditions passed along by word of mouth from one generation to the next.
- ◆ **Visual Materials** include paintings, drawings, sculptures, photographs, films, videos, and maps.
- ◆ **Artifacts** are objects such as tools, clothing, and money. Such objects tell about people's culture, customs, and technological development.
- ◆ **Personal Records** are accounts of events kept by eyewitnesses to the events. They include letters, diaries, and journals.
- ◆ **Poems and Songs** express the personal thoughts, beliefs, and feelings of the writer.
- ◆ **Printed Publications** include such items as newspapers, magazines, autobiographies, and books.

PRIMARY SOURCE FEATURES

A primary source quotation is included in nearly every chapter of the student edition. Background information about the quotation is included in the Teaching Strategies in this guide.

A primary source feature is included in each unit of the student edition. The primary source feature enhances and extends the material already covered in the chapter. Suggestions for using the primary source features are included in the Teaching Strategies in this guide.

A constructed response writing question is included at the end of each Primary Source Feature activity. For students, the question has been labeled, Think and Write. Constructed response questions are also known as document based questions. These types of questions measure the ability of a student to work with multiple perspectives on social studies issues. The constructed response questions may ask students to incorporate outside knowledge into their response.

INTRODUCTION AND EXPLANATION

Five Themes of Geography pages at the front of the book emphasize the fundamental themes of geography. These themes are Location, Place, Human-Environment Interaction, Movement, and Regions and were outlined in the *Guidelines for Geographic Education: Elementary and Secondary School* (Joint Committee on Geographic Education, 1984). These themes are the precursor to a more comprehensive framework set forth in the 1994 National Geography Standards volume, *Geography for Life*. The six elements in these standards are the World in Spatial Terms, Places and Regions, Physical Systems, Human Systems, Environment and Society, and the Uses of Geography. Although the trend in education is shifting away from the more popular five themes toward the six elements of geography, students at this level will benefit from learning and understanding geography skills by using the five themes.

The Using Maps questions throughout this book reinforce the five themes of geography.

Place is described by two kinds of features—physical features and human features. Physical features include such natural features as landforms, climate, plant life, animal life, altitude, and soil. Human features are those features created or developed by people, such as roads, buildings, land use, population, religion, and government. The features of a place make it unique. A generic blackline master for this theme is on page 116 of this guide. There are suggestions for its use in the Teaching Strategies in this guide.

Location is the position of people and places on Earth. Location can be described in two ways—absolute location and relative location. Absolute location is described using a specific address based on a grid system, such as a street address. Latitude and longitude give the absolute location of a place based on the intersection of lines of latitude and lines of longitude. Relative location describes a location in relation to what it is near or what is around it. One example of relative location is to give directions. (The shopping mall is northwest of your house.) A generic blackline master for this theme is on page 117 of this guide. There are suggestions for its use in the Teaching Strategies in this guide.

Movement is the study of the interdependence of people; the linkages between places; and the patterns of movement involving people, goods, information, and ideas. Movement describes the way people, goods, information, and ideas move from place to place. A generic blackline master for this theme is on page 118 of this guide. There are suggestions for its use in the Teaching Strategies in this guide.

Human/Environment Interaction describes relationships within places. It describes the interaction of people and their environment, such as the way people adapt to and depend upon their environment. For example, people in plains areas may use the land for grazing cattle or for growing crops. Another aspect of human/environment interaction is the way people change the environment to meet their needs and wants. For example, a coal company might strip the land to mine the coal in an area. Human/environment interaction includes the study of how technology impacts the environment. The damage to water supplies as a result of pollution is an issue studied in this theme. A generic blackline master for this theme is on page 119 of this guide. There are suggestions for its use in the Teaching Strategies in this guide.

Region is the basic unit of geographic study. Region is a way to organize information about places in an area with common features. Geographers use physical and human features as criteria to draw regional boundaries. Some physical features used include climate, landforms, bodies of water, and natural resources. Some human features used include land use, language, political units, government, and economics. Regions can be as small as a neighborhood or as large as a continent. A generic blackline master for this theme is on page 120 of this guide. There are suggestions for its use in the Teaching Strategies in this guide.

USING GEOGRAPHY THEMES FEATURES

A geography theme feature is included in each unit of the student edition. The geography theme feature enhances and extends the material already covered in the chapter. Suggestions for using the geography theme features are included in the Teaching Strategies in this guide.

TEACHING STRATEGIES

Summary: Long before our country was named the United States, Native Americans lived in America. About 500 years ago, people from Europe began to explore and settle America.

Major Concepts:
- **Geography:** European colonization of America led to various settlements in the Southwest and along the Atlantic Ocean and the Gulf of Mexico.
- **Government:** The Mayflower Compact was the first government in America that allowed people from Europe to rule themselves.
- **History:** When Europeans reached America, they began rapid colonization of the new land.
- **Sociology:** Native Americans and Africans were often forced by Europeans to work as slaves.

Pre-Reading Activities: **1.** Have students find Europe and North America on a globe or world map. Help them determine how far it is between the two continents. **2.** Ask students to list reasons why people might face a difficult journey when moving to another country. **3.** Have students look at the time line in the unit opener. Ask them to calculate about how many years of American history this unit covers. Then ask them to predict the main ideas of the unit based on the information in the unit time line, the title of the unit, and the picture in the unit opener.

Post-Reading Discussion Points: **1.** Ask students to make changes or additions to their list of reasons from Pre-Reading Activity 2 based on what they learned in this unit. **2.** Ask students what happened to Native Americans and Africans when Europeans began to settle in America. **3.** Discuss how today's communities still show the effects of early European settlement. Suggest that students think about the names of streets, businesses, and sports teams, as well as the last names of families, kinds of businesses, religions, languages, etc.

Follow-Up Activities: **1.** Give students the map of the United States on page 123 of this guide. Have students label or highlight the areas where English, French, and Spanish settlers lived. **2.** Use the Feature Chart graphic organizer on page 113 of this guide as a classroom activity. On the left, list *Spain, England,* and *France.* Across the top, write purposes and characteristics of explorer nations. For example, people from these nations may have searched for gold, traded for furs, or wanted religious freedom. See the sample of this graphic organizer in the *About the Program* section of this guide.

Review Activities: Refer to pages 18–19 of this guide for review activities covering this unit.

Assessment: Refer to pages 20–21 of this guide for the Unit Test.

ANSWER KEY

Unit Review (Bk 1 and CE, p. 37)
1. Florida **2.** Southwest **3.** Jamestown
4. Atlantic Ocean **5.** St. Lawrence **6.** Gulf of Mexico
7. New Orleans **8.** New France

Unit Review (Teacher's Guide, pp. 18–19)

Choose the Answer 1. 1492 **2.** La Salle
3. 1754 **4.** Cartier explored the St. Lawrence River for France.

Match Up 1. a **2.** d **3.** e **4.** c **5.** b

Riddle Review 1. corn **2.** Florida **3.** Pilgrims
4. turkeys **5.** Massasoit **6.** tobacco **7.** fur
8. Isabella
Answer: C O L U M B U S

Unit Test (Teacher's Guide, pp. 20–21)

True or False 1. T **2.** T **3.** F **4.** F **5.** T **6.** T

Match Up 1. c **2.** e **3.** b **4.** a **5.** d

Sequencing Events The sentences should be numbered 5, 3, 1, 4, 2.

Finish the Sentence 1. spices **2.** missions
3. La Salle **4.** Maryland **5.** Providence
6. England

TEACHING STRATEGIES

Summary: Native Americans in different parts of America lived according to the available resources.

Objective: Students will learn that Native Americans occupied America before Europeans arrived and that they developed different ways of living based on the resources available to them.

Pre-Reading Activities: 1. Have students compare a map or globe that shows the political borders of the United States to one that shows the North American landmass itself. Explain that Canada and Mexico are also part of North America. **2.** Ask students to describe what the chapter illustrations show about Native American life. **3.** Ask students to describe their state's environment. Discuss the importance of climate and natural resources in our everyday lives.

Vocabulary Activities: Write each vocabulary word on the chalkboard and discuss its meaning. Call on students to use each word correctly in a sentence.

Post-Reading Discussion Points: 1. Ask students to describe how Native Americans lived in different ways in different parts of the country. **2.** Have students describe some ways that Native Americans have helped other people in America.

Primary Source Quote: Luther Standing Bear was chief of the Ogala Sioux. He lived from 1905 to 1939.

ELL Activity: Help students trace the first Americans' route from Asia to the Americas on a map of the world. Students who came to the United States from another country may wish to label their country on the map and show or tell how they came to the United States.

Follow-Up Activities: 1. Give students the map of the United States on page 123 of this guide. Have students label each region of the United States as shown in the map on page 5.

Ask them to draw pictures on the map to show some of the natural resources in each region. For instance, they might draw buffalo in the Great Plains or corn in the Southwest. **2.** Have each student research the natural resources or the environment of a different state to suggest ways that Native Americans in that state might have lived. **3.** Use the Concept Web graphic organizer on page 109 of this guide to show information about Native Americans in the United States today. In the center of the concept web, write *Native Americans in the United States Today*. On the spokes of the concept web, have students write about what Native Americans in the United States do today.

Chapter Online Resources:
Find more information about topics in this chapter at *www.HarcourtAchieve.com/AchievementZone*. Click on *America's Story*.

ANSWER KEY

Learning from Pictures (Bk 1 and CE, p. 4)
They fished with nets.

Using What You've Learned

Choose a Word (Bk 1 and CE, p. 7)
1. Americans **2.** fishing **3.** corn **4.** buffalo
5. hunters **6.** medicines

Fact or Opinion (Bk 1 and CE, p. 7)
1. F **2.** F **3.** O **4.** F **5.** O **(CE) 6.** F

Understanding Continents (Bk 1 and CE, p. 8)
1. Asia, Africa, North America, South America, Antarctica, Europe, Australia **2.** North America
3. Asia **4.** Atlantic Ocean **(CE) 5.** Indian Ocean **(CE) 6.** South America

Journal Writing (Bk 1 and CE, p. 8)
Sentences will vary. Answers should identify where two groups of Native Americans lived and should list hunting, fishing, or farming as each group's means of getting food.

TEACHING STRATEGIES

Summary: Christopher Columbus attempted to find an easier way to travel from Europe to Asia by ship. Instead, he reached the land we call America.

Objective: Students will understand how the desire for trade with India and China led to Europeans reaching America.

Pre-Reading Activities: 1. Give students the world outline map on page 124 of this guide. Have them label North America, South America, Africa, Europe, Asia, India, China, Italy, Spain, and the Bahamas. Show students the lands that Columbus reached. 2. On a globe or a world map, tape a piece of paper over North America and South America to show that people from Europe did not know these lands existed. Show how Columbus thought he could reach Asia by sailing west across the Atlantic Ocean.

Vocabulary Activities: 1. Give examples of different kinds of spices. 2. Discuss the meaning of *New World.* Explain that America already existed, but it seemed new to the European explorers who had not known about it.

Post-Reading Discussion Points: 1. Ask students why Queen Isabella gave Columbus three ships. 2. Ask students why they think Columbus was willing to go on a long, dangerous voyage. Why do people today go into space?

Primary Source Quote: By October 15, 1492 Columbus and his crew had been sailing without sight of land for over two months.

ELL Activity: Have students work in groups to write a one-act play about what they think the journey to the Americas was like for Columbus and the members of his crew. Have each group perform their play in front of the class.

Follow-Up Activities: 1. Have students research one spice to find out where it comes from and how it is used. 2. Have students debate the following proposition: If Columbus had not made his voyage, North America and South America would never have been reached by Europeans. 3. Ask students to describe how the Native American way of life might have been different if Columbus had not reached America.

Chapter Online Resources:
Find more information about topics in this chapter at *www.HarcourtAchieve.com/AchievementZone.* Click on *America's Story.*

ANSWER KEY

Learning from Pictures (Bk 1 and CE, p. 9)
Answers will vary, but may include relieved, grateful, happy, and thankful.

Using Maps (Bk 1 and CE, p. 11)
Bahama Islands and Hispaniola

Using What You've Learned

Choose the Answer (Bk 1 and CE, p. 12)
1. to get jewels, silks, and spices   2. India
3. ships   4. Atlantic Ocean   5. 1492

Using Graphic Organizers: Main Idea and Supporting Details (Bk 1 and CE, p. 12)
1. People traveled to India and China to get jewels and spices.
2. When Columbus landed in America, he thought he was in India.

Using Map Directions (Bk 1 and CE, p. 13)
1. east   2. west   3. south   4. north   5. east   6. west

TEACHING STRATEGIES

Summary: Spain sent people to America to find gold and to teach the Native Americans to become Catholics.

Objective: Students will learn some of the effects of Spain's 300 years of colonial rule in America.

Pre-Reading Activities: **1.** Explain that since Spanish soldiers found gold in South America and Mexico, they believed they could find gold in other parts of North America. Ask students why it might have been important to the Spanish to find gold. **2.** Have students compare the map on page 15 to a map that shows the modern political borders of the United States. Ask them to tell in which states the Spanish searched for gold.

Vocabulary Activities: **1.** Have students work in pairs calling out the new words to each other as spelling words. **2.** Have students draw pictures that show the meaning of the words *slavery, missions,* and *priests.* Ask students to write sentences using each of these words.

Review Words: religions, claimed, cotton

Post-Reading Discussion Points: **1.** Ask students what they think the Spanish might have done if they had found the seven cities of gold. **2.** Ask students to compare the success of the Spanish mission priests with the success of the explorers searching for gold. **3.** Ask students which people may have suffered as a result of Spanish exploration in America.

Primary Source Quote: Father Serra sent this letter dated July 3, 1769 to his future biographer, Father Palu.

ELL Activity: Have pairs of students choose an explorer and work cooperatively to learn all they can about their explorer from the textbook and other sources. Then have each pair of students take turns answering *yes* or *no* as other pairs of students ask questions to discover the explorer's name. If a student cannot answer a question, have him or her work with their partner to find the answer.

Geography Theme Activities: Have students write a paragraph about the city or community where they live. The paragraph should include information about the land, plants, and weather. It should tell about the

people who live there and what has been built there. Have students take or locate photographs of the city or community. Have them find maps of the city or community. Have students read their paragraphs to the class and share their photographs and maps. Then discuss how the place where they live is different from Santa Fe, New Mexico.

Follow-Up Activities: **1.** Have each student research another Spanish explorer, such as Francisco Pizarro, Juan Ponce de León, or Hernando Cortés. Have each student share what he or she learned about the explorer with the class. **2.** Have students research the story of Estevanico. Ask them to tell the story to the class, explaining how an African became an explorer for the Spanish.

Chapter Online Resources:
Find more information about topics in this chapter at *www.HarcourtAchieve.com/AchievementZone.* Click on *America's Story.*

ANSWER KEY

Learning from Pictures (Bk 1 and CE, p. 14)
There is a cactus in the picture.

Using Maps (Bk 1 and CE, p. 15)
north and east

Using Geography Themes (Bk 1 and CE, p. 17)
1. the Southwest **2.** Sangre de Cristo Mountains **3.** bricks of dried mud **4.** many Pueblo Indians **5.** Santa Fe River **6.** Students should list two of the following: San Miguel Mission, Palace of the Governors, State Capitol.

Using What You've Learned

Finish the Sentence (Bk 1 and CE, p. 18)
1. Estevanico **2.** Southwest **3.** Florida **4.** Mississippi River **5.** seven **6.** missions **(CE) 7.** 300

Categories (Bk 1 and CE, pp. 18–19)
1. Francisco Coronado **2.** King of Spain **3.** Explorers **4.** Hernando de Soto

Using a Map Key (Bk 1 and CE, p. 19)
1. Spanish missions **2.** City **3.** Spanish land **4.** De Soto's route

1. 7 **2.** 4 **3.** Mississippi **4.** east **5.** south

TEACHING STRATEGIES

Summary: The Pilgrims came to America because they wanted freedom of religion. The Wampanoag helped the Pilgrims through the first hard year.

Objective: Students will learn why the Pilgrims left England and how the Wampanoag helped the Pilgrims survive in Plymouth, Massachusetts.

Pre-Reading Activities: 1. Have students describe how the picture on page 20 shows that the Pilgrims had a hard trip to America. **2.** Ask students to look at the other chapter illustrations. Have them describe each picture and ask them what they think they will learn from the chapter.

Vocabulary Activities: 1. Discuss the meanings of the words *compact* and *treaty*. **2.** Write sentences on the chalkboard, leaving a blank where each new word should go. Have students decide which new word should go in each blank.

Review Words: religions

Post-Reading Discussion Points: 1. Ask students why they think the Pilgrims went to Holland first instead of coming straight to America. **2.** Have students list problems the Pilgrims might have faced in moving to Holland and later to America. Ask students to compare the Pilgrims' move to America to that of immigrants today.

ELL Activity: Using the words in Chapter 4, write a poster-sized cloze passage about the Pilgrims' experiences in America. Read the passage with students and model how to use contextual clues to fill in the blanks. Give each student a card with a word that completes a blank in the passage. Read the passage again and have students add their words.

Follow-Up Activities: 1. Have students research the foods served at the first Thanksgiving dinner. Have them write a paragraph comparing these foods to the ones traditionally served at Thanksgiving today. **2.** Have students use the Cause and Effect graphic organizer on page 111 of this guide in a cooperative learning activity. Have students enter the following causes into the Cause column of their Graphic organizer: 1. The Pilgrims wanted freedom of religion. 2. The first winter in Plymouth was very cold. 3. Massasoit signed a peace treaty with the Pilgrims. Then have students complete the effects column.

Chapter Online Resources:
Find more information about topics in this chapter at *www.HarcourtAchieve.com/AchievementZone*. Click on *America's Story*.

ANSWER KEY

Learning from Pictures (Bk 1 and CE, p. 20)
They were going to settle in America and build a colony. (Bk 1 and CE, p. 21) fish

Using What You've Learned

Choose the Answer (Bk 1 and CE, p. 23)
1. England **2.** to have freedom of religion
3. *Mayflower* **4.** Plymouth

Cause and Effect (Bk 1 and CE, p. 23)
1. d **2.** e **3.** a **4.** b **5.** c

Reading a Flow Chart (Bk 1 and CE, p. 24)
1. clear away **2.** fish **3.** squash **4.** store

Journal Writing (Bk 1 and CE, p. 24)
Paragraphs will vary. Answers might include three or more of the following: They had a lot of food. The Wampanoag had helped them. They believed God had helped them. Plymouth was growing. They wouldn't be hungry that winter. They had freedom of religion in America. They ruled themselves. They had peace with the Wampanoag.

TEACHING STRATEGIES

Summary: English people began coming to America in 1585. By 1753 there were 13 English colonies along the Atlantic Ocean.

Objective: Students will understand the reasons for the settlement of English colonies in America. They will learn how Africans and Native Americans participated in that settlement.

Pre-Reading Activities: 1. Help students make a class chart of reasons why people might leave their homes to move to a relatively unknown land. **2.** Ask students why they think freedom of religion was so important that people would take a dangerous trip to a new land in order to have this freedom.

Vocabulary Activities: 1. Write each new word on an index card or a piece of paper. Shuffle the cards and have students draw for words. Have each student write their word on the chalkboard and then pronounce it. **2.** Have students write a sentence using each vocabulary word.

Review Words: religions, freedom of religion, Church of England, slavery

Post-Reading Discussion Points: 1. Ask students why they think the Puritans came to America for freedom of religion but would not give the same right to other people. **2.** Discuss how Africans and Native Americans participated in the settlement of the 13 English colonies.

Primary Source Activities: 1. Ask students to name some things that are primary sources. **2.** Have students make a time capsule containing primary sources that would help people in the future learn about their lives.

ELL Activity: Divide students into groups. Have each group use a wall map of the United States to locate the cities where the English settled. Ask each group to choose one location and list facts about the English who settled there.

Follow-Up Activities: 1. Read students the story of Pocahontas and Captain John Smith. Have students put on a short play telling the story.

Chapter Online Resources:
Find more information about topics in this chapter at *www.HarcourtAchieve.com/AchievementZone.* Click on *America's Story.*

ANSWER KEY

Learning from Pictures (Bk 1 and CE, p. 25)
They took their supplies off the boat, chopped down trees, and built homes.

Using Primary Sources (Bk 1 and CE, p. 28)
1. A coin was found. **2.** an ink jar **3.** They put them in candle holders and used them for light at night. **4.** fish and turtles **5. Constructed Response** Answers will vary. Students should point out that although they have changed, coins, fish hooks, and candle holders are still used today. Turtles are still used for food in some cultures and pens no longer need to be filled with ink from a jar.

Using What You've Learned

Write the Answer (Bk 1 and CE, p. 29)
1. English people came to get rich, for freedom of religion, and to have a better life. **2.** Captured Africans were brought to help grow tobacco. **3.** The Puritans came for freedom of religion. **(CE) 4.** The Puritans started the first schools in America. **(CE) 5.** The first city was Providence, Rhode Island. **(CE) 6.** James Oglethorpe brought people who were in debt in England to Georgia.

Using Graphic Organizers: Sequencing Events (Bk 1 and CE, p. 29)
1. The English started Jamestown, their first town in America. **2.** The Puritans started a colony in Massachusetts in 1628. **3.** Roger Williams and Anne Hutchinson left Massachusetts to have freedom of religion. **4.** In 1681 William Penn started the peaceful colony of Pennsylvania.

Journal Writing (Bk 1 and CE, p. 29)
Paragraphs will vary. Answers should identify one of the 13 English colonies and explain reasons why the student would choose to live in that colony.

Reading a Historical Map (Bk 1 and CE, p. 30)
1. Virginia **2.** Georgia **3.** New Hampshire **4.** Pennsylvania

TEACHING STRATEGIES

Summary: French people came to America to find a water route to Asia, to find furs, and to teach Native Americans to be Catholics. England and France fought a war over who should own land in America.

Objective: Students will understand why French people settled in America, what the relationship between the French and the Native Americans was like, and how France lost most of its American land to England.

Pre-Reading Activities: 1. Help students create a chart with the columns *Spanish, English,* and *French* and the rows *Reasons for Coming to America* and *Help from Native Americans.* Have students fill in the chart for the Spanish and English columns. Tell students they will complete the French column after they read the chapter. 2. Help students locate the St. Lawrence River, the Mississippi River, Canada, St. Louis, New Orleans, and the Gulf of Mexico on a map.

Vocabulary Activities: Have students write a sentence using each word.

Review Words: colony, slavery, freedom of religion, religions, settlers

Post-Reading Discussion Points: 1. Tell students to complete the French column of the chart they created in Pre-Reading Activity 1. Ask students to compare the information in the three columns. 2. Have students discuss how their lives might be different today if France had won the French and Indian War.

Primary Source Quote: Hennepin is describing the scenery of the Detroit River. He thought it was more beautiful than that of the Niagara.

ELL Activity: Have student pairs use the textbook and other resources to learn more about the French in America. Then have the pairs create a poster about what they learned.

Follow-Up Activities: 1. Have students write a paragraph on how Native Americans might have felt about English, Spanish, and French settlers claiming land in America. 2. Have students use the Sequencing graphic organizer on page 110 of this guide to show how the French explored, settled, fought battles, and lost land in America. 3. Help students use the Geography Theme: Place blackline master on page 116 of this guide to describe New France. Tell students to use the information in Chapter 6, the map on page 33, and any outside resources to help them complete this activity.

Chapter Online Resources:
Find more information about topics in this chapter at *www.HarcourtAchieve.com/AchievementZone.* Click on *America's Story.*

ANSWER KEY

Learning from Pictures (Bk 1 and CE, p. 31)
Native Americans

Using Maps (Bk 1 and CE, p. 33)
the St. Lawrence River and the Mississippi River

Using What You've Learned

Finish the Story (Bk 1 and CE, p. 35)
1. Mississippi 2. Louisiana 3. furs 4. Catholic
5. canoes 6. French

Fact or Opinion (Bk 1 and CE, p. 35)
1. F 2. F 3. O 4. F 5. F 6. F 7. O 8. O 9. O
10. F

Using Map Directions (Bk 1 and CE, p. 36)
1. northeast 2. east 3. west 4. southeast 5. east
6. south

Name _____

◄ UNIT REVIEW ►

THE SETTLERS OF AMERICA

Choose the Answer   Use the time line from the unit opener to answer the questions below. Draw a circle around the correct answer.

1. In what year did Columbus reach America?
   1492   1540   1733

2. Who explored the Mississippi River in 1682?
   Cartier   Coronado   La Salle

3. When did the French and Indian War begin?
   1534   1619   1754

4. Which event happened before the English started Jamestown, Virginia?
   England won the French and Indian War.
   Cartier explored the St. Lawrence River for France.
   Captured Africans were brought to Jamestown.

Match Up   Finish each sentence in Group A with words from Group B. Write the letter of the correct answer on the blank line.

Group A

1. _____ started a Quaker colony in Pennsylvania.

2. Native Americans in different parts of the United States spoke different _____ .

3. After the French and Indian War, England owned _____ .

4. Christopher Columbus wanted to find an easier way to _____ .

5. The Spanish built many _____ in the Southwest.

Group B

a. William Penn

b. missions

c. Asia

d. languages

e. Canada

Name _____

◄ UNIT REVIEW ►
THE SETTLERS OF AMERICA

Riddle Review   Use a word in dark print to complete each sentence below. Write the word on the blanks next to each sentence.

Florida	corn	Isabella	Pilgrims
Massasoit	fur	tobacco	turkeys

1. Native Americans of the Southwest grew _____ and beans for their families.
☐ _ _ _

2. Hernando de Soto went to _____ .
_ _ ☐ _ _ _ _

3. The _____ went to Holland to have freedom of religion.
_ _ ☐ _ _ _ _ _

4. Native Americans of the East killed deer and _____ for food.
_ ☐ _ _ _ _ _

5. _____ made a peace treaty with the Pilgrims in Plymouth.
☐ _ _ _ _ _ _ _ _

6. English settlers in Jamestown grew _____ .
_ _ ☐ _ _ _ _

7. Native Americans taught the French how to trap animals for _____ .
_ ☐ _

8. Queen _____ gave ships to Columbus.
_ ☐ _ _ _ _ _ _

The letters in the boxes spell a word. The word answers the riddle.

RIDDLE: Who had a city in the state of Ohio named after him?

ANSWER: _ _ _ _ _ _ _ _

Name _____

◖ UNIT TEST ◗
THE SETTLERS OF AMERICA

True or False Write **T** next to each sentence that is true. Write **F** next to each sentence that is false.

_____ 1. Columbus claimed America for Spain.

_____ 2. The settlers in Jamestown brought captured Africans to help them grow tobacco.

_____ 3. Cartier was a Dutch explorer who searched for the seven cities of gold.

_____ 4. Most French people came to America because they wanted freedom of religion.

_____ 5. Native Americans made their tools out of animal bones and stones.

_____ 6. The Mayflower Compact said that the Pilgrims would make laws that were fair to all.

Match Up Finish each sentence in Group A with words from Group B. Write the letter of the correct answer on the blank line.

Group A

1. The flat land in the Midwest of the United States is called the _____ .

2. Native Americans are sometimes called _____ .

3. An African who explored the Southwest for Spain was _____ .

4. The _____ came to Massachusetts for freedom of religion.

5. French settlers learned how to use _____ from Native Americans.

Group B

a. Puritans

b. Estevanico

c. Great Plains

d. snowshoes

e. American Indians

© Steck-Vaughn Company

Name _____

◀ UNIT TEST ▶

THE SETTLERS OF AMERICA

Sequencing Events   Write the numbers **1, 2, 3, 4,** and **5** next to these sentences to show the correct order.

_____   France lost the French and Indian War in 1763.

_____   Francisco Coronado looked for gold in the Southwest in 1540.

_____   Native Americans were the first people to live in America.

_____   James Oglethorpe started the Georgia colony in 1733 for people in English jails.

_____   Columbus claimed America for Spain.

Finish the Sentence   Draw a circle around the word or words that finish each sentence.

1. People from Europe went to India and China to get jewels, silks, and _____ .
   corn   buffalo skins   spices

2. The Spanish built _____ because they wanted the Native Americans to become Catholics.
   stores   missions   schools

3. _____ sailed down the Mississippi River to the Gulf of Mexico.
   Columbus   La Salle   Massasoit

4. The _____ colony was started so Catholics could have freedom of religion.
   Maryland   Georgia   Rhode Island

5. Roger Williams started _____ , where there was freedom of religion for all.
   Plymouth   Jamestown   Providence

6. France fought with _____ during the French and Indian War.
   Spain   England   Africa

TEACHING STRATEGIES

Summary: American colonists fought for and won their independence from Great Britain in the American Revolution. People such as Benjamin Franklin and George Washington contributed to the creation of the new government of the United States of America.

Major Concepts:
◆ **Government:** The United States Constitution and government were created so that Americans could help write laws.
◆ **History:** The American Revolution began as colonists protested unfair laws passed by the British government.
◆ **Sociology:** The lives of important individuals, such as Benjamin Franklin and George Washington, offer insight into their contributions to American history.

Pre-Reading Activities: 1. Ask students how they would feel if another government took over the United States. Would students be willing to follow the laws of another government? What might they do to change the situation? **2.** Have students tell what they know about the American government. List these ideas on the chalkboard or a piece of paper so that students can refer to them during the study of this unit. **3.** Have students look at the time line in the unit opener. Ask them to calculate about how many years of American history this unit covers. Then ask them to predict the main ideas of the unit based on the information in the unit time line, the title of the unit, and the picture in the unit opener.

Post-Reading Discussion Points: 1. Ask students to review the list made in Pre-Reading Activity 2. Have them make changes or additions based on what they learned in this unit. **2.** Have students tell how different groups of people contributed to the American Revolution. **3.** Ask students to discuss George Washington's and Benjamin Franklin's contributions to America.

Follow-Up Activities: 1. Have students research the contributions of other leaders, such as Samuel Adams, Patrick Henry, and Thomas Paine. How did they contribute to the American Revolution? **2.** Have students use the Event Description graphic organizer on page 114 of this guide to show important information about the American Revolution. In the center box have students write *American Revolution*. Then have students complete the rest of the organizer. **3.** Have students read parts of the annotated Declaration of Independence found on pages 322–326 and The Constitution of the United States of America found on pages 327–354 aloud.

Review Activities: Refer to pages 28–29 of this guide for review activities covering this unit.

Assessment: Refer to pages 30–31 of this guide for the Unit Test.

ANSWER KEY

Unit Review (Bk 1 and CE, p. 71)
1. Boston **2.** Philadelphia **3.** Trenton **4.** Yorktown **5.** New York City **6.** Washington, D.C.

Unit Review (Teacher's Guide, pp. 28–29)

Choose the Answer 1. the Bill of Rights **2.** 1773 **3.** George Washington died. **4.** 1781

Match Up 1. b **2.** d **3.** a **4.** e **5.** c

Riddle Review 1. Declaration **2.** Capitol **3.** Lady **4.** vote **5.** Benjamin **6.** African **7.** chief **8.** justices
Answer: C O L O N I E S

Unit Test (Teacher's Guide, pp. 30–31)

True or False 1. T **2.** T **3.** F **4.** F **5.** F **6.** T

Match Up 1. e **2.** c **3.** d **4.** b **5.** a

Sequencing Events The sentences should be numbered 3, 4, 1, 5, 2.

Finish the Sentence 1. Parliament **2.** send tax money to Great Britain **3.** Declaration of Independence **4.** giving money **5.** Capitol **6.** plan Washington, D.C.

TEACHING STRATEGIES

Summary: Great Britain passed many laws that the people in the 13 colonies did not like. In 1775 the Americans living in the colonies began a war to win more freedom from Great Britain.

Objective: Students will understand the causes of the American Revolution.

Pre-Reading Activities: **1.** Have students look at the picture on page 42. How are the men on the ships dressed? What are they doing? **2.** Ask students how they might feel if they did not have a vote in decisions that affect them. What might they do to change such a situation? **3.** Explain that England is part of Great Britain and that the government of Great Britain is called the British government.

Vocabulary Activities: Write each vocabulary word on the chalkboard and discuss its meaning. Call on students to use each word correctly in a complete sentence.

Review Words: colony

Post-Reading Discussion Points: **1.** Help students make a chart showing some of the reasons that Americans wanted freedom from Great Britain. **2.** Ask students if they think it was fair for the colonists to pay taxes for the cost of defense during the French and Indian War. **3.** Ask students why they think the Americans called throwing tea into the ocean at Boston a tea party. How did the British react to the Boston Tea Party? How did King George respond?

Primary Source Quote: This quote is from a letter John Adams wrote to H. Niles dated February 13, 1818.

ELL Activity: Assign three-year time periods from 1760 to 1775 to student groups. Groups should use the textbook to find events in that time period that led to the American Revolution. Have groups record and illustrate events on a class time line.

Follow-Up Activities: **1.** Have students role-play a meeting in which colonists decide to have the Boston Tea Party. Have students argue for and against having the event. **2.** Use the Cause and Effect graphic organizer on page 112 of this guide as a group activity. Have students enter the following causes into the cause column of their graphic organizer: 1. The British wanted the colonies to help pay for the French and Indian War. 2. Americans did not like the Stamp Act. 3. The British made a law that said Americans must pay a tea tax. Then have students complete the effects column.

Chapter Online Resources:
Find more information about topics in this chapter at *www.HarcourtAchieve.com/AchievementZone.* Click on *America's Story.*

ANSWER KEY

Learning from Pictures (Bk 1 and CE, p. 42)
to show that they supported throwing the tea into the Atlantic Ocean

Using What You've Learned

Match Up (Bk 1 and CE, p. 44)
1. c **2.** e **3.** d **4.** a **5.** b

Understanding Different Points of View
(Bk 1 and CE, pp. 44–45)
1. British **2.** American **3.** American **4.** British
5. British **6.** American

Reading a Time Line (Bk 1 and CE, p. 45)
1. 1774 **2.** 1776 **3.** 1763 **4.** 1765 **5.** 1773

Journal Writing (Bk 1 and CE, p. 45)
Paragraphs will vary. Students should explain why they would want to help the Americans or the British.

TEACHING STRATEGIES

Summary: Many groups of people helped America win its independence from Great Britain in the American Revolution.

Objective: Students will learn about the Declaration of Independence and about the people who helped America win its independence.

Pre-Reading Activities: **1.** Ask students why Great Britain might have wanted to keep its colonies. **2.** Have students pretend they are going to fight a war to start a new country. Have them list the things they would need to do to prepare for the war.

Vocabulary Activities: Write the new words on pieces of paper so that each student can pick a word from a box. They must use the word correctly in an oral sentence.

Review Words: American Revolution, Parliament, nation, colony, peace treaty, freedom of religion

Post-Reading Discussion Points: **1.** Have students tell about some of the people involved in the American Revolution. **2.** Ask students to tell how their lives might be different today if America had not won the American Revolution. **3.** Have students turn to the Declaration of Independence on page 322. Discuss the statement "All men are created equal." Ask students if they think all people in America were truly equal in 1776. Do they think all people are equal in America today?

Primary Source Activities: **1.** Explain to students that besides diaries, primary sources include journals, newspapers, letters, and other documents. Tell the students that the Declaration of Independence is an example of a primary source. **2.** Find other examples of primary sources from the time period of the American Revolution. Read and discuss these primary sources with the students.

ELL Activity: Assign sections of the Declaration of Independence to student pairs. Have each pair read their section, look up unfamiliar words, and explain the section to the class.

Follow-Up Activities: **1.** Have students research and report on the life story of a person who signed the Declaration of Independence. **2.** Use the Sequencing graphic organizer on page 110 of this guide in cooperative learning groups. Have students list the major events of the struggle for American independence.

Chapter Online Resources:
Find more information about topics in this chapter at *www.HarcourtAchieve.com/AchievementZone*. Click on *America's Story*.

ANSWER KEY

Learning from Pictures (Bk 1 and CE, p. 47)
Answers will vary, but may include huddling around a fire, trying to cook something to eat, and wrapping themselves in extra clothing. (Bk 1 and CE, p. 48) She loaded cannons.

Using Primary Sources (Bk 1 and CE, p. 50)
1. march over the river **2.** It was full of burnt leaves and dirt. **3.** His shoes were worn out, and his shirt hung in strings. **4.** December 18 **5. Constructed Response:** Answers will vary. Students should point out that the winter at Valley Forge was hard for the soldiers because the weather was cold and snowy. The soldiers had poor food and clothing.

Using What You've Learned

Finish the Sentence (Bk 1 and CE, p. 51)
1. 1776 **2.** Philadelphia **3.** Friedrich von Steuben **4.** James Armistead **5.** 1781

True or False (Bk 1 and CE, p. 51)
1. T **2.** T **3.** F **4.** T **5.** F

Journal Writing (Bk 1 and CE, p. 51)
Answers will vary. News stories should explain that colonists wrote the Declaration of Independence to tell the world that the colonies no longer belonged to Great Britain. Students should include at least two of the following from the Declaration of Independence: "All men are created equal," all people should have freedom, and the 13 colonies were an independent nation.

Drawing Conclusions (Bk 1 and CE, p. 52)
1. d **2.** c **3.** a **4.** e **5.** b

TEACHING STRATEGIES

Summary: Benjamin Franklin was an important man to the city of Philadelphia and to the United States of America.

Objective: Students will learn about Benjamin Franklin's life and the contributions he made to the United States.

Pre-Reading Activities: **1.** Invite students to describe what the chapter illustrations tell them about Benjamin Franklin's life. **2.** Ask students to list some electrical appliances that make their lives easier. Ask them to tell what they know about electricity.

Vocabulary Activities: **1.** Discuss the meanings of the words in the New Words list. Have students write a paragraph that uses the words *printer, printing shop,* and *published.* **2.** Call on students to use the term *electric sparks* in a sentence.

Review Words: colony, Parliament, Stamp Act, tax, Declaration of Independence, American Revolution, independent

Post-Reading Discussion Points: **1.** Ask students to discuss how working at a newspaper might have influenced Benjamin Franklin's feelings about the need for freedom of the press. **2.** Have students discuss how Franklin's experience with newspapers might have made him a good person to deal with other countries and to help write the Declaration of Independence and the Constitution.

Primary Source Quote: This quote is from Benjamin Franklin's *Poor Richard's Almanac.*

ELL Activity: Have students look up *saying* and *proverb* in a dictionary. Share some of Benjamin Franklin's sayings with students and discuss possible interpretations. Have students write and illustrate their own sayings to share with the class.

Follow-Up Activities: **1.** Have students research Franklin's inventions and his contributions to Philadelphia and the United States. Have them report their findings to the class. **2.** If possible, take the class to view a modern–day newspaper publisher. How is today's printing and publishing process different from that of Benjamin Franklin's time?

Chapter Online Resources:
Find more information about topics in this chapter at *www.HarcourtAchieve.com/AchievementZone.* Click on *America's Story.*

ANSWER KEY

Learning from Pictures (Bk 1 and CE, p. 53)
Answers will vary, but may include newspapers, books, posters, advertisements, and calendars.

Using What You've Learned

Find the Answers (Bk 1 and CE, p. 56)
Students should choose the following sentences:
2. Franklin started a hospital and a public library in Philadelphia.
3. Franklin started a fire department in Philadelphia.
4. Franklin helped Thomas Jefferson write the Declaration of Independence.
6. Franklin helped write the Constitution in 1787.

Using Graphic Organizers: Cause and Effect
(Bk 1 and CE, p. 56)
1. c **2.** b **3.** a

Reading a Bar Graph (Bk 1 and CE, p. 57)
1. 15,000 **2.** 34,000 **3.** 22,000 **4.** Philadelphia
5. Boston

Journal Writing (Bk 1 and CE, p. 57)
Paragraphs will vary. Students may mention any of the following about Benjamin Franklin: published a newspaper; started Philadelphia's first fire department, first public library, and a school; worked with electricity; signed the Declaration of Independence; went to France to get help; helped write the Constitution; helped Philadelphia become a great city; and helped the United States become a free country.

TEACHING STRATEGIES

Summary: George Washington served his country as soldier, commander in chief, and President.

Objective: Students will learn about George Washington's life and the contributions he and Martha Washington made to the United States.

Pre-Reading Activities: **1.** Have students list qualities they think a good leader should have. Tell students to look for these qualities in George Washington as they read. **2.** Show several portraits of Washington from various books or other sources. Ask students what the artists did to show that Washington was a great man.

Vocabulary Activities: Ask students to read in the text the sentences in which the bold-faced vocabulary words appear. Have them use the context of the sentences to guess what each word means.

Review Words: general, colony, independent, American Revolution, peace treaty, Constitution, slavery, nation, surrendered, capital

Post-Reading Discussion Points: **1.** Ask students how American soldiers could win the revolution when they did not have enough food, clothes, or guns. **2.** Ask students how the statement "First in war, first in peace, first in the hearts of his countrymen" applies to George Washington. **3.** Ask students what work Martha Washington might have done as First Lady. How might her work have been different from that of today's First Lady?

Geography Theme Activities: **1.** Help students find the location of their community on a county or state map. Ask students to describe the location of their community using directions and describing what it is near or what is around it. **2.** Have students find Washington, D.C., on a map of the United States. Ask them to describe its location in the United States.

Primary Source Quote: Washington accepted his appointment as commander in chief of the army at the Second Continental Congress.

ELL Activity: Ask students to form into groups. Assign each group a topic from the textbook pertaining to George Washington's life. Topics might include childhood, commander in chief, Constitutional Convention, and President. Have each group create a drawing that illustrates their topic based on what they learned.

Follow-Up Activities: **1.** Assign students to research different aspects of Washington's career. Help students create a time line. **2.** Have students use the Concept Web graphic organizer on page 109 of this guide to summarize Washington's important contributions. Write *George Washington* in the center. On the spokes, ask students to write what Washington did for his country.

Chapter Online Resources:
Find more information about topics in this chapter at *www.HarcourtAchieve.com/AchievementZone*. Click on *America's Story*.

ANSWER KEY

Learning from Pictures (Bk 1 and CE, p. 61)
Answers will vary, but may include that he is promising to be a good President, he is giving a speech, and he is being sworn into office.

Using Geography Themes (Bk 1 and CE, p. 63)
1. Maryland and Virginia **2.** the Potomac River **3.** Maryland **4.** Chesapeake Bay **5.** south **6.** Answers will vary. Students should tell about the location of Washington, D.C., using directions, what it is near, and what is around it.

Using What You've Learned

Finish the Sentence (Bk 1 and CE, p. 64)
1. manage **2.** French and Indian **3.** commander in chief **4.** New York City **5.** Trenton **6.** the Constitutional Convention **7.** First Lady **8.** Benjamin Banneker

Sequencing Events (Bk 1 and CE, p. 64)
(Bk 1) 2, 5, 3, 4, 1 **(CE) 1.** Washington helped the British win the French and Indian War. **2.** General Washington led the American army during the revolution. **3.** The British army surrendered to George Washington in Yorktown. **4.** George Washington helped write the Constitution. **5.** George Washington became the first President of the United States.

TEACHING STRATEGIES

Summary: The early leaders of America created the Constitution and the Bill of Rights to give Americans many rights and freedoms.

Objective: Students will understand the basic form of government set up by the Constitution.

Pre-Reading Activities: **1.** Discuss what it would be like if there were no laws. **2.** Ask students if they know who the President is and who represents them in Congress. Ask students to tell what they know about their state and city governments, as well as rule-making groups such as school boards.

Vocabulary Activities: **1.** Have students write each word and say it correctly. **2.** Use the Concept Web graphic organizer on page 109 of this guide. Write *United States Government* in the center. On the surrounding spokes, students should write vocabulary words that are associated with government.

Review Words: American Revolution, colony, independent, capital, Constitution, Constitutional Convention, Parliament, freedom of religion

Post-Reading Discussion Points: **1.** Ask students why the new United States needed a constitution. Have them explain why the writers of the Constitution used Parliament as a guide. **2.** Have students discuss how Americans help write laws. **3.** Ask students to look at the diagram on page 67. Ask them to explain the powers of each branch of government.

ELL Activity: Have student groups investigate how the Constitution affects areas of their lives such as safety, the media, housing, jobs, and religion. To show what they learned, groups might create bulletin boards of the pages for a class book.

Follow-Up Activities: **1.** Ask students to turn to the Constitution of the United States of America on page 327. Have each student choose a different section or amendment of the Constitution and report its meaning to the class. **2.** Have students write and mail letters to their senators or representatives in Congress. Tell them to express their opinions about a current issue. **3.** Help students navigate the website *http://bensguide.gpo.gov* to learn more about our government. The link "Election Process" helps explain the role of the electoral college in a presidential election. Guide students through the events of the 2000 election to show how George W. Bush was elected President.

Chapter Online Resources: Find more information about topics in this chapter at *www.HarcourtAchieve.com/AchievementZone*. Click on *America's Story*.

ANSWER KEY

Learning from Pictures (Bk 1 and CE, p. 65) Answers will vary, but may include that a leader was in charge, a secretary made a record of the meeting, the discussion was lively, and the participants cared about the subject.

Using What You've Learned

Write the Answer (Bk 1 and CE, p. 69) **1.** American leaders wrote the Constitution at the Constitutional Convention in Philadelphia. **2.** Senators and representatives write our country's laws. **3.** Each state has two senators in the United States Senate. **4.** The President carries out the country's laws and helps make our country's laws. **(CE) 5.** The White House, Capitol, and Supreme Court buildings are in Washington, D.C. **(CE) 6.** The Constitution did not give Americans certain freedoms and rights. **(CE) 7.** The Bill of Rights added freedom of religion, freedom of the press, and other freedoms. **(CE) 8.** Our Constitution now has 27 amendments.

Using Graphic Organizers: Main Idea and Supporting Details (Bk 1 and CE, pp. 69–70) **1.** Americans made a constitution that said they could help write their own laws. **2.** The Constitution says Americans can choose people to work in their government. **3.** The United States government has three branches.

Reading a Diagram (Bk 1 and CE, p. 70) **1.** three **2.** President **3.** nine **4.** senators **5.** 435 **6.** 100

Journal Writing (CE, p. 70) Answers will vary. Students should write that Americans wrote in the Constitution that Americans should vote for people to work for them in the government. Americans help write their own laws by voting for senators and representatives who write laws in Congress. Americans also vote for the President, who carries out the laws.

Name _____

◀ UNIT REVIEW ▶
BUILDING A NEW COUNTRY

Choose the Answer   Use the time line from the unit opener to answer the questions below. Draw a circle around the correct answer.

1. What was written in 1791?
   the Declaration of Independence   the Constitution   the Bill of Rights

2. In what year was the Boston Tea Party?
   1765   1770   1773

3. What happened in 1799?
   George Washington finished his work as President.
   George Washington died.
   George Washington became America's first President.

4. When did America win the American Revolution?
   1775   1781   1787

Match Up   Finish each sentence in Group A with words from Group B. Write the letter of the correct answer on the blank line.

Group A

1. Great Britain made Americans pay taxes to help pay for the _____ .

2. The Americans surprised the British at _____ on Christmas.

3. The British would not let Americans write laws in _____ .

4. The Senate and the House of Representatives are the two houses of _____ .

5. Benjamin Franklin asked _____ to help Americans fight against the British.

Group B

a. Parliament

b. French and Indian War

c. France

d. Trenton, New Jersey

e. Congress

Name _____

◀ UNIT REVIEW ▶
BUILDING A NEW COUNTRY

Riddle Review   Use a word in dark print to complete each sentence below. Write the word on the blanks next to each sentence.

| **Capitol** | **chief** | **Declaration** | **African** |
| vote | Lady | Benjamin | justices |

1. The _____ of Independence was written in 1776.

   _ _ □ _ _ _ _ _ _ _ _ _ _

2. Congress meets in the _____ building.

   _ _ _ _ _ □ _

3. Martha Washington was the First _____ .

   □ _ _ _

4. Americans _____ for their leaders.

   _ □ _ _

5. _____ Franklin used a kite to learn more about electricity.

   _ _ □ _ _ _ _ _

6. _____ American soldiers fought against the British in the American Revolution.

   _ _ _ □ _ _ _

7. George Washington was commander in _____ of the American army.

   _ _ _ □ _

8. Supreme Court _____ decide whether laws agree with the Constitution.

   _ _ □ _ _ _ _ _

The letters in the boxes spell a word. The word answers the riddle.

RIDDLE: Where can both settlers and ants live?

ANSWER: _ _ _ _ _ _ _ _ _

Name _____

◢ UNIT TEST ◣

BUILDING A NEW COUNTRY

True or False   Write **T** next to each sentence that is true. Write **F** next to each sentence that is false.

_____ 1. Great Britain made a new tax law called the Stamp Act that said Americans had to pay tax on things made from paper such as newspapers.

_____ 2. The Boston Tea Party made King George very angry.

_____ 3. Benjamin Franklin fought as a soldier in the American Revolution.

_____ 4. After the American Revolution, the United States had 23 states.

_____ 5. The Bill of Rights says that senators and representatives write our country's laws.

_____ 6. The British army surrendered to General George Washington at Yorktown, Virginia.

Match Up   Finish each sentence in Group A with words from Group B. Write the letter of the correct answer on the blank line.

Group A

1. The American war against Great Britain was called the _____ .

2. The _____ was written in 1776.

3. Every state has _____ senators in Congress.

4. The man who showed that lightning is a kind of electricity was _____ .

5. The first President of the United States was _____ .

Group B

a. George Washington

b. Benjamin Franklin

c. Declaration of Independence

d. two

e. American Revolution

Name _____

◁ UNIT TEST ▷

BUILDING A NEW COUNTRY

Sequencing Events   Write the numbers **1**, **2**, **3**, **4**, and **5** next to these sentences to show the correct order.

_____   The 13 colonies became independent when Great Britain lost the American Revolution in 1781.

_____   Benjamin Franklin helped write the Constitution.

_____   Americans threw tea into the ocean in 1773 because they did not like the tea tax.

_____   George Washington became the first President in 1789.

_____   Thomas Jefferson helped write the Declaration of Independence in 1776.

Finish the Sentence   Draw a circle around the word or words that finish each sentence.

1. American colonists wanted to send their own leaders to help write laws in the British _____ .
   Congress   Parliament   Supreme Court

2. To pay for the French and Indian War, the British government made a law that said Americans had to _____ .
   drink tea   send tax money to Great Britain   close the port of Boston

3. "All men are created equal" is part of the _____ .
   Declaration of Independence   Bill of Rights   Constitution

4. Haym Salomon helped the American army by _____ .
   becoming a soldier   asking the French to help   giving money

5. The Senate and the House of Representatives meet in the _____ building.
   Supreme Court   White House   Capitol

6. Benjamin Banneker used math and science to _____ .
   make electricity   plan Washington, D.C.   print newspapers

TEACHING STRATEGIES

Summary: During the 1800s the United States showed the world its growing strength as it sought more land, defended its rights, and changed as a result of the Industrial Revolution. During this time thousands of Native Americans were forced to move to land west of the Mississippi River. Throughout this time many Americans worked to improve life in America.

Major Concepts:
- **Civics:** Americans worked to end slavery and fight for women's rights.
- **Economics:** The Industrial Revolution caused goods to be made faster and cheaper.
- **Geography:** Americans' desire for more land led to the Louisiana Purchase and to conflicts with Native Americans.
- **History:** The War of 1812 showed Great Britain and the world that the United States was a strong nation.
- **Sociology:** Native Americans were forced to move to Indian Territory. As the American population increased, there was a growing need for more public schools and a desire for better education for women.

Pre-Reading Activities: **1.** Ask students how a settler in the early 1800s might have traveled from the Atlantic coast to the Pacific coast. How might one travel this distance today? **2.** Have students use the map on page 76 to study the borders between areas owned by the United States, Spain, and Great Britain. Then, show students the map of the United States on page 123 of this guide. Ask students what they think happened to change the size of the United States. **3.** Have students look at the time line in the unit opener. Ask them to calculate about how many years of American history this unit covers. Then ask them to predict the main ideas of the unit based on the information in the unit time line, the title of the unit, and the picture in the unit opener.

Post-Reading Discussion Points: **1.** Ask students why it might be important to a nation such as the United States to gain more land instead of remaining a small country. **2.** Ask students to list some of the

important individuals in American history during the 1800s. Have them tell what each person did.

Follow-Up Activities: **1.** Help students use the Feature Chart graphic organizer on page 113 of this guide to compare and contrast the treatment of white men, Native Americans, African Americans, and women. **2.** Encourage students to learn more about the history of education in the United States. What other groups have had limited educational opportunities?

Review Activities: Refer to pages 38–39 of this guide for review activities covering this unit.

Assessment: Refer to pages 40–41 of this guide for the Unit Test.

ANSWER KEY

Unit Review (Bk 1 and CE, p. 107)
1. doubled **2.** Louisiana **3.** 1812 **4.** Cherokee **5.** Industrial Revolution **6.** factory **7.** cities **8.** reform **9.** women's rights

Unit Review (Teacher's Guide, pp. 38–39)

Choose the Answer 1. 1804 **2.** Great Britain **3.** 1825 **4.** The Cherokee were forced to move west.

Match Up 1. c **2.** e **3.** d **4.** a **5.** b

Riddle Review 1. painting **2.** seas **3.** lawyers **4.** canals **5.** Cherokee **6.** women **7.** York Answer: T E A C H E R

Unit Test (Teacher's Guide, pp. 40–41)

True or False 1. T **2.** F **3.** F **4.** T **5.** T **6.** T

Match Up 1. c **2.** b **3.** e **4.** d **5.** a

Sequencing Events The sentences should be numbered 4, 1, 5, 2, 3.

Finish the Sentence 1. New York City **2.** New Orleans **3.** Sequoyah **4.** Spain **5.** Dorothea Dix **6.** Andrew Jackson

TEACHING STRATEGIES

Summary: In 1803 the United States bought Louisiana from France. The Louisiana Purchase doubled the size of the United States. Lewis and Clark explored Louisiana and traveled to the Pacific Ocean. Lewis and Clark, along with Sacagawea and York, helped Americans learn about the land in the West.

Objective: Students will understand the importance of the Louisiana Purchase to the United States. Students will also learn about the journey of Lewis and Clark.

Pre-Reading Activities: 1. Help students find New Orleans and the Mississippi River on the map on page 76. Ask them to compare the area included in the Louisiana Purchase with the modern state of Louisiana. Clarify any confusion about the use of the name. **2.** Have students look at the pictures on pages 74 and 77. Ask students what conclusions they can draw about Lewis and Clark's trip to explore the Louisiana Purchase.

Vocabulary Activities: Discuss the meaning of each of the vocabulary words. Have students write sentences using each word.

Review Words: port, Declaration of Independence, American Revolution, settlers, nation, slavery

Post-Reading Discussion Points: 1. Discuss why the Mississippi River and New Orleans were so important to American farmers. Ask students to consider the importance of water transportation in America in a time when there were few roads. **2.** Ask students what they think might have happened to Lewis and Clark's expedition without help from Sacagawea and York.

Primary Source Quote: By November 1805 Lewis and Clark, 18 months after their journey began, arrived at the Pacific Ocean.

ELL Activity: Have student groups read more of Clark's description of his journey through the land of the Louisiana Purchase. Have groups choose one description from Clark's journal and depict it in a drawing.

Follow-Up Activities: 1. Help students use the Sequencing graphic organizer on page 110 of this guide to show which nations have owned Louisiana. Remind students how Spain got Louisiana from France in the French and Indian War. **2.** Help students use the Geography Theme: Place blackline master on page 116 of this guide to describe New Orleans in 1803. Tell students to use the photo of New Orleans on page 75, the map on page 76, and any outside resources to help them complete this activity.

Chapter Online Resources:
Find more information about topics in this chapter at *www.HarcourtAchieve.com/AchievementZone.* Click on *America's Story.*

ANSWER KEY

Learning from Pictures (Bk 1 and CE, p. 74)
Because she was familiar with the area and they were not.

Using Maps (Bk 1 and CE, p. 76)
St. Louis

Using What You've Learned

True or False (Bk 1 and CE, p. 78)
1. F **2.** F **3.** T **4.** T **5.** F **6.** T **7.** T

Reviewing Map Directions (Bk 1 and CE, p. 78)
1. west **2.** north **3.** east **4.** south **5.** northwest
6. southeast

Categories (Bk 1 and CE, p. 79)
1. Jefferson **2.** Napoleon Bonaparte **3.** Louisiana
4. Lewis and Clark **(CE) 5.** York **(CE) 6.** Sacagawea

Journal Writing (Bk 1 and CE, p. 79)
Paragraphs will vary. Five items from the list should be identified with reasons why each item would have been important on Lewis and Clark's journey.

TEACHING STRATEGIES

Summary: In 1812 America fought Great Britain over freedom of the seas. The war showed that the United States was strong enough to protect its rights.

Objective: Students will understand the causes and results of the War of 1812.

Pre-Reading Activities: 1. Ask students how they would feel if British captains forced them to sail and work on British ships. **2.** Have students look at the picture on page 82. Ask if they knew that Washington, D.C., had been burned by another country's army.

Vocabulary Activities: 1. Ask students to use the meaning of *freedom of the press* to infer the meaning of *freedom of the seas*. **2.** Have each student write a short paragraph using all of the new vocabulary words.

Review Words: capital, First Lady, port, general, peace treaty

Post-Reading Discussion Points: 1. Ask students how freedom of the seas is still important to the United States. Suggest that they think about where America gets most of its oil and what could happen if the supply of oil was stopped. **2.** Ask students if they feel that Tecumseh was right in fighting for the British in the War of 1812. **3.** Ask students how the Battle of New Orleans might have been affected if the telephone or telegraph had been invented before the war.

Primary Source Quote: In a letter to her sister dated August 23, 1814, Dolley Madison describes her last moments in the White House before the British Army burns it.

ELL Activity: Have students use their pupil edition to create a class time line about the War of 1812. Encourage students to draw pictures of events on the time line.

Primary Source Activities: 1. Have students role play Tecumseh and Governor Harrison. **2.** Find other speeches by Native Americans regarding the treaties they were forced to sign with the United States government. Read and discuss these with the students.

Follow-Up Activities: 1. Help students use the Cause and Effect graphic organizer on page 111 of this guide to show the causes and effects of the War of

1812. **2.** Have students read biographies of Dolley or James Madison. **3.** Have students work in groups to make a time line of events in the chapter.

Chapter Online Resources:
Find more information about topics in this chapter at *www.HarcourtAchieve.com/AchievementZone*. Click on *America's Story*.

ANSWER KEY

Learning from Pictures (Bk 1 and CE, p. 80)
the ship on the right, which is the American ship because it has an American flag

Using Primary Sources (Bk 1 and CE, p. 84)
1. chief of the Shawnee **2.** Governor William Henry Harrison **3.** the Great Spirit **4.** white people
5. Constructed Response He said that Native Americans were happy; because they were there first and had a right to the land until they chose to leave it

Using What You've Learned

Choose the Answer (Bk 1 and CE, p. 85)
1. France **2.** freedom of the seas **3.** James Madison **4.** Tecumseh **5.** to get back Native American lands **6.** Dolley Madison **7.** the United States **8.** Francis Scott Key **9.** Andrew Jackson

Journal Writing (Bk 1 and CE, p. 85)
Paragraphs will vary. Answers should reflect the writer's understanding that Jackson had just fought a battle where many lives were lost only to learn that it was unnecessary. Students will likely say that Jackson was angry, sad, upset, etc.

Drawing Conclusions (Bk 1 and CE, p. 86)
1. b **2.** d **3.** a **4.** c

Sequencing Events (CE, p. 86)
The sentences should be in the following order:
1. The British forced many Americans to work on British ships. **2.** The United States began to fight Great Britain for freedom of the seas. **3.** The British burned Washington, D.C. **4.** Great Britain and the United States signed a peace treaty. **5.** Andrew Jackson won the Battle of New Orleans.

TEACHING STRATEGIES

Summary: The Industrial Revolution brought many changes to American life. Samuel Slater built a factory in the United States for spinning thread. Inventions and new ideas for making goods helped the Industrial Revolution expand. The Industrial Revolution caused America to grow.

Objective: Students will learn about the beginning of the Industrial Revolution and the inventions and new ideas that helped it grow. They will also learn how the Industrial Revolution caused change in the United States.

Pre-Reading Activities: **1.** Ask students to name inventions in communication and transportation. Have the students discuss how these inventions changed peoples' ways of life. **2.** Have students look at the pictures and read the captions in this chapter. Ask them to name some of the inventions that will be discussed in the chapter.

Vocabulary Activities: Have students choose a vocabulary word from the list of new words and draw a picture of it. Ask them to write a caption for their picture using the vocabulary word in the caption. Ask students to share their pictures and read their captions to the class.

Review Words: cotton

Post-Reading Discussion Points: **1.** Have students discuss how the Industrial Revolution began in the United States. **2.** Discuss how canals, steamboats, railroads, and locomotives helped the growth of the Industrial Revolution in the United States. Ask the students to identify other inventions and new ideas that helped the Industrial Revolution. **3.** Have students compare and contrast life in the United States before and after the Industrial Revolution. Ask them how life changed for Americans.

Primary Source Quote: By 1810 the steamboat was such a success that others started to copy Fulton's model.

ELL Activity: Show students the photo of the cotton gin on page 88 of the pupil edition. Encourage them to guess its purpose. After revealing the cotton gin's

purpose, ask students to think of inventions that have made a difference in the way we live today.

Follow-Up Activities: **1.** Have the students write *The Industrial Revolution* in the center box of the Event Description graphic organizer on page 114 of this guide. Have students complete the rest of the information on the graphic organizer.

Chapter Online Resources:
Find more information about topics in this chapter at *www.HarcourtAchieve.com/AchievementZone.* Click on *America's Story.*

ANSWER KEY

Learning from Pictures (Bk 1 and CE, p. 87)
Answers will vary. Workers did not wear safety equipment. They could get their hands or clothes caught in the machines.

Using What You've Learned

Find the Answers (Bk 1 and CE, p. 91)
Students should choose the following sentences:
1. In the 1700s the British invented machines that changed how cloth was made. **2.** Samuel Slater built spinning machines in the United States. **4.** Mass production made it faster and cheaper to make goods.

Using Graphic Organizers: Cause and Effect
(Bk 1 and CE, p. 91)
1. b **2.** a **3.** c

Journal Writing (Bk 1 and CE, p. 91)
Paragraphs will vary. Students should write about two ways the United States changed as a result of the Industrial Revolution. Students may mention that before the revolution, goods were made by hand at home. After the revolution most goods were made by machines in factories. The way goods were made was changed by inventions such as the cotton gin and by new ideas, such as mass production. Goods became cheaper. Many people became factory workers. Better ways to move goods and people were invented. Cities grew. Fewer people lived and worked on farms.

Reading a Line Graph (Bk 1 and CE, p. 92)
1. 96,000 **2.** 1830 **3.** move to the city **4.** grew larger **5.** 313,000

TEACHING STRATEGIES

Summary: Andrew Jackson believed Americans should have Native American lands. Congress passed a law that forced Native Americans to move to Indian Territory west of the Mississippi River.

Objective: Students will learn about Andrew Jackson's career and the importance of Sequoyah and Osceola in Native American history.

Pre-Reading Activities: 1. Point out the pictures of Sequoyah and Osceola on pages 94 and 96. Ask students how these Native Americans are different from Native Americans often shown in old Western movies.   **2.** Have students discuss whether it would be easy or hard to invent a new alphabet.

Vocabulary Activities: Help students compare the meanings of *border* and *tariffs* with the meanings of *boundary* and *taxes.* Discuss with students how they can use different words to express a similar meaning.

Review Words: American Revolution, surrendered, Congress, captured, tax

Post-Reading Discussion Points: 1. Ask students how they would feel if people from another part of the country forced them to move from their home state. **2.** Discuss why Jackson forced South Carolina to pay tariffs for the goods from Europe. Ask students why it is necessary for all states to obey the laws of the United States.

Primary Source Quote: The alphabet that Sequoyah created for the Cherokee language uses 85 symbols.

ELL Activity: Have student pairs use the pupil edition and other resources to learn more about Andrew Jackson. Then have pairs create a poster about what they learned.

Geography Theme Activities: 1. Discuss the geography theme of movement with the students. Ask students to identify all the ways they get from one place to another. Then ask students to identify all the ways they learn about new ideas.   **2.** Have students study the picture on page 97. Ask students: Do the Native Americans look happy about this move? What kinds of things did the Native Americans take with them? How did they travel? Was the trip easy or difficult? How do you know?

Follow-Up Activities: 1. Have students research and report on the Cherokee nation, including how the Cherokee live today.   **2.** Have students write *Andrew Jackson* in the center of the Concept Web graphic organizer on page 109 of this guide. On the spokes, have them write information about Jackson's life and career.

Chapter Online Resources:
Find more information about topics in this chapter at *www.HarcourtAchieve.com/AchievementZone.* Click on *America's Story.*

ANSWER KEY

Learning from Pictures (Bk 1 and CE, p. 95)
about 177 years old

Using Geography Themes (Bk 1 and CE, p. 98)
1. They walked or traveled in wagons.   **2.** boats
3. from the Cherokee adults who brought the stories to Indian Territory   **4.** Students should list five of the following states: Alabama, Tennessee, Kentucky, Illinois, Missouri, Arkansas, and Oklahoma.
5. Mississippi River, Arkansas River, and Tennessee River

Using What You've Learned

Finish the Story (Bk 1 and CE, p. 99)
1. Creek   **2.** Florida   **3.** Spain   **4.** five   **5.** tariff
6. Territory   **7.** Trail of Tears   **8.** Cherokee   **9.** alphabet
10. newspaper   **11.** Osceola   **12.** west   **13.** Army
14. Florida

Fact or Opinion (Bk 1 and CE, p. 100)
1. F   **2.** O   **3.** F   **4.** O   **5.** F   **6.** O   **7.** F   **8.** F   **9.** F
10. F   **11.** F   **12.** O   **13.** O   **14.** O

Journal Writing (Bk 1 and CE, p. 100)
Sentences will vary. Answers should reflect students' understanding of the frustration, anger, sadness, fear, etc., that Native Americans who were forced to move west might have felt.

TEACHING STRATEGIES

Summary: Many groups of Americans in the United States were treated unfairly. Americans worked for reform to end these unfair treatments. They worked to improve public schools, end slavery, reform jails, and gain rights for women.

Objective: Students will learn how people in the United States worked to improve the country.

Pre-Reading Activities: **1.** Have students read the questions in *Find Out* on page 101. Ask them to identify the main ideas of this chapter. **2.** Ask students whether all people should have the same educational opportunities.

Vocabulary Activities: Write each vocabulary word on the chalkboard and discuss its meaning. Call on students to use each word correctly in a complete sentence.

Review Words: slavery, published

Post-Reading Discussion Points: **1.** Discuss the fact that many people did not think women were able to learn the same subjects as men. Ask students if they see any evidence today that such ideas still exist. **2.** Ask students if they think most Americans today have equal opportunities. **3.** Ask students why Horace Mann worked to have the state of Massachusetts pay for children to go to public schools.

Primary Source Quotes: 1. Frederick Douglass worked for an end to slavery and for equal treatment of African Americans. 2. Elizabeth Cady Stanton is describing what happened at a convention to discuss the rights of women in 1848.

ELL Activity: Discuss with students how abolitionists and reformers in the 1800s worked to change their society. Have students choose a problem in their community or state and help them write a letter to a person who can help, such as a city council member or a company president. You might prepare a letter of your own for students to use as a model.

Follow-Up Activities: **1.** Ask students to research such women as Emma Willard, Elizabeth Blackwell, Lucy Stone, Sarah and Angelina Grimké, or Lucretia Mott. **2.** Have students use the Cause and Effect graphic organizer on page 111 of this guide to show how reformers in the early 1800s helped improve the country. Ask them how the reformer's actions affect students today.

Chapter Online Resources:
Find more information about topics in this chapter at *www.HarcourtAchieve.com/AchievementZone.* Click on *America's Story.*

ANSWER KEY

Learning from Pictures (Bk 1 and CE, p. 103)
Boston, Massachusetts

Using What You've Learned

Match Up (Bk 1 and CE, p. 105)
1. c **2.** b **3.** d **4.** a

Finding the Main Idea (Bk 1 and CE, p. 105)
1. There were problems in American education in the 1800s.
2. Girls did not get the same education that boys did.
3. People tried to help girls get a better education.
4. Some Americans wanted to end slavery.

Reading a Chart (Bk 1 and CE, p. 106)
1. top to bottom **2.** left to right **3.** Horace Mann
4. Frederick Douglass **5.** women's rights

Name _____

◁ UNIT REVIEW ▷

THE UNITED STATES GROWS

Choose the Answer Use the time line from the unit opener to answer the questions below. Draw a circle around the correct answer.

1. Lewis and Clark began to explore Louisiana in what year?
   1801   1803   1804

2. The United States and what country signed a peace treaty in 1814?
   France   Great Britain   Spain

3. In what year was the Erie Canal completed?
   1804   1820   1825

4. What happened after Andrew Jackson became President?
   The Cherokee were forced to move west.
   Sequoyah made the first Native American alphabet.
   The War of 1812 began.

Match Up Finish each sentence in Group A with words from Group B. Write the letter of the correct answer on the blank line.

Group A

1. _____ led Lewis and Clark to the Pacific Ocean.

2. The United States bought the Louisiana Purchase from _____ .

3. Many goods were made by machines in factories after the _____ .

4. During the War of 1812, the United States tried to capture _____ .

5. When the Cherokee were forced to move west, their journey was called the _____ .

Group B

a. Canada

b. Trail of Tears

c. Sacagawea

d. Industrial Revolution

e. France

Name _____

◀ UNIT REVIEW ▶
THE UNITED STATES GROWS

Riddle Review   Use a word in dark print to complete each sentence below. Write the word on the blanks next to each sentence.

seas	**painting**	**Cherokee**	**lawyers**
York	**women**	**canals**	

1. Dolley Madison saved the _____ of George Washington during the War of 1812.

   _ _ _ _ □ _ _ _

2. America wanted freedom of the _____ .

   _ □ _ _ _

3. In the early 1800s, women could not become _____ .

   _ □ _ _ _ _ _ _

4. Americans built _____ to move goods.

   □ _ _ _ _ _ _

5. Sequoyah made an alphabet for the _____ language.

   _ □ _ _ _ _ _ _ _

6. Mary Lyon started a college for _____ .

   _ _ _ □ _

7. _____ was an African American who helped Lewis and Clark.

   _ _ □ _

The letters in the boxes spell a word. The word answers the riddle.

RIDDLE: What did a one-room school in the early 1800s have that is still found in schools today?

ANSWER: _ _ _ _ _ _ _ _

Name _____

◁ UNIT TEST ▷

THE UNITED STATES GROWS

True or False   Write **T** next to each sentence that is true. Write **F** next to each sentence that is false.

_____ 1. Lewis, Clark, York, and Sacagawea explored the land of the Louisiana Purchase for Thomas Jefferson.

_____ 2. The United States fought for freedom of religion during the War of 1812.

_____ 3. Mass production slowed down the making of goods.

_____ 4. British soldiers burned Washington, D.C., during the War of 1812.

_____ 5. William Lloyd Garrison worked to end slavery.

_____ 6. Andrew Jackson said that all states must obey the laws of the United States.

Match Up   Finish each sentence in Group A with words from Group B. Write the letter of the correct answer on the blank line.

Group A

1. As the United States grew larger, many _____ were forced to leave their lands.

2. A man named _____ helped Lewis and Clark explore the West.

3. _____ was President of the United States during the War of 1812.

4. The leader of the Seminole in Florida was _____ .

5. _____ worked to improve women's education.

Group B

a. Mary Lyon

b. York

c. Native Americans

d. Osceola

e. James Madison

Name _____

◁ UNIT TEST ▷
THE UNITED STATES GROWS

Sequencing Events   Write the numbers **1**, **2**, **3**, **4**, and **5** next to these sentences to show the correct order.

_____   Andrew Jackson became President in 1829.

_____   The Industrial Revolution began in the United States in 1790.

_____   The Cherokee were forced to move to Oklahoma in 1838.

_____   The United States bought Louisiana from France.

_____   The United States fought Great Britain for freedom of the seas.

Finish the Sentence   Draw a circle around the word or words that finish each sentence.

1. The Erie Canal helped _____ become a very large city.
   Washington, D.C.   Santa Fe   New York City

2. Thomas Jefferson wanted the United States to own _____ .
   New Orleans   Oregon   Canada

3. _____ was a Cherokee who helped his people learn to read and write.
   Tecumseh   Osceola   Sequoyah

4. In 1819 _____ sold Florida to the United States.
   Great Britain   France   Spain

5. _____ worked for reform in American jails.
   Thomas Gallaudet   Dorothea Dix   Elizabeth Cady Stanton

6. _____ won the Battle of New Orleans in 1815.
   Andrew Jackson   Thomas Jefferson   Francis Scott Key

TEACHING STRATEGIES

Summary: As the United States expanded west, the nation faced increasing conflicts with other nations and between its own states.

Major Concepts:
- **Economics:** The northern states were more industrialized than the southern states. Southern states had less money to fund the Civil War.
- **Geography:** The idea of Manifest Destiny led to westward expansion of the United States.
- **History:** The issue of slavery led to hostility between the northern and southern states and caused the Civil War.
- **Sociology:** Americans in Texas defended their rights to make their own laws, have freedom of religion, and speak their own language in Mexico.

Pre-Reading Activities: **1.** Have students describe what is happening in the picture on pages 108–109. Tell students that during the mid-1800s the United States faced conflicts between its own states and with Mexico. **2.** Ask students if they know what the word *Union* means. Explain that this word sometimes refers to the United States. **3.** Discuss the history of American slavery.

Post-Reading Discussion Points: **1.** Ask students to compare and contrast the way Texas and the Mexican Cession were added to the United States with the way Oregon Country was added. **2.** Have students explain the causes of the Civil War. Ask students what it might have been like if the United States had remained divided.

Follow-Up Activities: **1.** Help students use the Feature Chart graphic organizer on page 113 of this guide to compare the four areas of land obtained by the United States in the 1800s. **2.** Invite students to research the effects of the Civil War on a southern city, such as Atlanta, Savannah, Vicksburg, Richmond, or Charleston.

Review Activities: Refer to pages 48–49 of this guide for review activities covering this unit. Refer to page 52 for a time line review covering Bk 1 and CE, Units 1–4.

Assessment: Refer to pages 50–51 of this guide for the Unit Test. Refer to pages 53–54 for the Final Test covering Bk 1 and CE, Units 1–4.

ANSWER KEY

Unit Review (Bk 1, p. 144; CE, p. 145)
1. Texas **2.** state **3.** Cession **4.** California **5.** Confederate **6.** Civil War **7.** slaves **8.** Lee **9.** Lincoln

Unit Review (Teacher's Guide, pp. 48–49)

Choose the Answer 1. 1821 **2.** 1850 **3.** The Civil War ended. **4.** 1846 **5.** Texas

Match Up 1. d **2.** c **3.** e **4.** a **5.** b

Riddle Review 1. property **2.** Confederate **3.** James **4.** Mexico **5.** Alamo **6.** Abraham **7.** Cession **8.** Richmond
Answer: R E M E M B E R

Unit Test (Teacher's Guide, pp. 50–51)

True or False 1. T **2.** F **3.** F **4.** F **5.** T **6.** T

Match Up 1. c **2.** e **3.** d **4.** a **5.** b

Sequencing Events The sentences should be numbered 5, 2, 1, 3, 4.

Finish the Sentence 1. Manifest Destiny **2.** own property **3.** six months **4.** James Beckwourth **5.** North **6.** Union

Time Line Review covering Bk 1/CE Units 1–4 (Teacher's Guide, p. 52)
The correct order, top to bottom, is j, g, e, a, h, c, f, b, i, d.

Final Test covering Bk 1/CE Units 1–4 (Teacher's Guide, pp. 53–54)

True or False 1. F **2.** T **3.** F **4.** T **5.** T **6.** F

Match Up 1. c **2.** d **3.** e **4.** b **5.** a

Sequencing Events The sentences should be numbered 4, 3, 1, 5, 2.

Finish the Sentence 1. vote for their President, senators, and representatives **2.** George Washington **3.** west of the Mississippi River **4.** Declaration of Independence **5.** South **6.** Industrial Revolution

TEACHING STRATEGIES

Summary: In 1821 Americans began to settle in Texas, which was part of Mexico. In 1836 Texans fought for and won the freedom to start their own independent country.

Objective: Students will understand the causes and main events of the Texas Revolution.

Pre-Reading Activities: 1. Have students compare the area of Texas as shown on the map on page 113 to a map showing the modern state of Texas. **2.** Ask students to recall some of the reasons that Americans wrote the Declaration of Independence. Tell them that many people who lived in Texas wanted freedom from Mexico, so they also wrote a declaration of independence.

Vocabulary Activities: 1. Help students use their understanding of the term *American Revolution* to infer the meaning of *Texas Revolution*. **2.** Help students pronounce each Hispanic name correctly. Explain that the pronunciation of many Hispanic names has been Americanized. For example, San Jacinto (SAHN Ha SEEN toh) is often pronounced SAN Juh SIN toh in Texas.

Review Words: independent, settlers, Constitution, commander in chief, Declaration of Independence, colony, surrendered, slavery, missions

Post-Reading Discussion Points: 1. Ask students if they think Mexico was right to expect the Texans to obey Mexican laws. **2.** Ask students to compare the problems between Texas and Mexico to the problems between the 13 colonies and Great Britain.

ELL Activity: Have students create a mural. Tell students that the mural should show Santa Anna's surrender after the battle at the San Jacinto River, and the raising of the Texas Flag.

Primary Source Activities: 1. Review the definitions of the words in blue print with the students. **2.** Have students discuss the excerpts from William Barrett Travis's letters on page 114. Ask the students if Travis seems brave or scared, hopeful or discouraged. **3.** Find other primary sources about Texas settlement or the Texas Revolution. Read them to the class and discuss how these primary sources help people learn what happened during this time period.

Follow-Up Activities: 1. Have students use the Sequencing graphic organizer on page 108 of this guide to list the events leading to the creation of the Texas Republic. Have students use the graphic organizer to write a paragraph that summarizes the events. **2.** Ask students to research Stephen F. Austin, Suzanna Dickenson, Sam Houston, José Antonio Navarro, or Lorenzo de Zavala.

Chapter Online Resources:
Find more information about topics in this chapter at *www.HarcourtAchieve.com/AchievementZone*. Click on *America's Story*.

ANSWER KEY

Learning from Pictures (Bk 1 and CE, p. 110)
by covered wagon, by horse, and on foot

Using Primary Sources (Bk 1 and CE, p. 114)
1. in the Alamo **2.** send men **3.** surrender **4.** 10 days **5. Constructed Response** Answers will vary. Students should point out that Travis and the Texan soldiers were willing to fight because they believed that Texas should be free and independent from Mexican rule.

Using What You've Learned

Choose a Word (Bk 1 and CE, p. 115)
1. Stephen F. Austin **2.** Santa Anna **3.** Alamo
4. de Zavala **5.** Sam Houston **6.** Texas Revolution

Understanding Different Points of View
(Bk 1 and CE, p. 115)
1. Mexican **2.** Texan **3.** Mexican **4.** Texan
5. Texan **6.** Mexican **7.** Mexican **8.** Texan

TEACHING STRATEGIES

Summary: In 1845 Congress voted for Texas to become a state. Mexico challenged the Texas boundaries in a war with the United States. The United Stated gained lands to the Pacific Ocean.

Objective: Students will learn how the idea of Manifest Destiny and the admission of Texas to the United States led to war with Mexico and to the growth of the United States.

Pre-Reading Activities: 1. Ask students to look at the map on page 117. Explain that Mexico did not agree that Texas had much land north of the Rio Grande.   **2.** Have students list Hispanic influences in their lives. Suggest food, clothing, and place names. **3.** Help students locate the places from the People & Places list on page 116.

Vocabulary Activities: 1. Invite students to guess at meanings for the words *citizens* and *property* and explain their guesses.   **2.** Discuss the meaning of the term *Manifest Destiny*. Explain that this idea led to much of the expansion of the United States in the 1800s.

Review Words: peace treaty, capital, surrendered, border, republic, Congress, captured

Post-Reading Discussion Points: 1. Ask students to tell how Manifest Destiny helped the United States grow to its present size.   **2.** Ask students how people might feel if their capital city was captured by another nation during a war. Use the capture of Washington, D.C., in the War of 1812 and the capture of Mexico City during the Mexican War as examples.

Primary Source Quote: James K. Polk spoke these words in a message to Congress in 1945.

ELL Activity: Have students work in groups. Tell each group to pick a subject discussed in the chapter and write an article about it. Students should draw a picture to go with their article. When each group has completed their article, join the articles to resemble a newspaper. Have volunteers read articles from the newspaper to the class.

Follow-Up Activities: 1. Have students work in groups to provide food and music for a Mexican fiesta.   **2.** Show students a map that shows the

route of the Southern Pacific Railroad across the Southwest. Ask students why a railroad might be important to a growing nation.   **3.** Help students use the Geography Theme: Location blackline master on page 117 of this guide to locate one of the new lands gained by the United States in the mid-1800s. Use the map on page 118 or outside resources to help complete this activity.

Chapter Online Resources:
Find more information about topics in this chapter at *www.HarcourtAchieve.com/AchievementZone.* Click on *America's Story.*

ANSWER KEY

Using Maps (Bk 1 and CE, p. 118)
Mexican Cession

Learning from Pictures (Bk 1 and CE, p. 119)
Answers will vary, but may include that cowboys wore a hat, a jacket, chaps, and boots with spurs. They also carried a scarf.

Using What You've Learned

Choose the Answer (Bk 1 and CE, p. 120)
1. James K. Polk   **2.** 1845   **3.** Mexico City   **4.** Rio Grande   **5.** $15 million   **6.** California, Nevada, Arizona   **7.** Gadsden Purchase   **8.** for a railroad

Reviewing Map Directions (Bk 1 and CE, pp. 120–121)
1. north   **2.** west   **3.** east   **4.** south   **5.** east

Using Graphic Organizers: Cause and Effect (Bk 1 and CE, p. 121)
1. d   **2.** b   **3.** c   **4.** a

Journal Writing (Bk 1 and CE, p. 121)
Answers will vary. Paragraphs should list some of the contributions made by Mexican Americans, including bringing foods and music, helping change property laws to allow women to own property, sharing knowledge about growing food in dry conditions, helping build railroads, helping find gold and silver, and teaching Americans to be cowboys.

TEACHING STRATEGIES

Summary: Many Americans moved west in the 1840s and 1850s. Some started farms in Oregon. Others moved to California to look for gold.

Objective: Students will understand the reasons people moved west in the 1840s and 1850s.

Pre-Reading Activities: **1.** Ask students to study the pictures on pages 124 and 125. What do these pictures tell about the settlers in the West and the lives they led? **2.** Help students locate on a wall map the endpoint of a 2,000-mile-long journey that begins from their town.

Vocabulary Activities: Have students work in pairs to write sentences for the new words, using the glossary of *America's Story* as needed.

Review Words: Manifest Destiny, settlers, nation, Congress

Post-Reading Discussion Points: **1.** Ask students why so many people moved to Oregon and California. **2.** Discuss how the gold rush and the Beckwourth Pass affected the settling of California and its admission as a state.

Primary Source Quote: The letters and journal of Narcissa Whitman span from March to December of 1836. She was the first white woman to travel on the Oregon Trail.

ELL Activity: Explain to students that before families could travel west they would have to prepare for their journey. They would need to bring along with them everything they would need to survive the journey and to start a new life in the West. Have students work in small groups. Tell students to make a list of what they would need if they were traveling by covered wagon across the country to start a new life.

Geography Theme Activities: **1.** Have students review the definitions of the vocabulary words in the feature. **2.** Ask students to describe the environment in which they live, describing ways in which people have changed that environment.

Follow-Up Activities: **1.** Ask students to research how James Beckwourth or Levi Strauss helped prospectors during the California gold rush. **2.** Have students use the Event Description graphic organizer on page 114 of this guide. Have students write *Gold Rush* in the center box of the organizer and complete the rest of the information.

Chapter Online Resources:
Find more information about topics in this chapter at *www.HarcourtAchieve.com/AchievementZone.* Click on *America's Story.*

ANSWER KEY

Learning from Pictures (Bk 1 and CE, p. 122)
Answers will vary, but may include that families sometimes had to push their wagons over steep mountain passes.

Using Maps (Bk 1 and CE, p. 123)
Answers will vary, but may include that they created paths that others could use, and they used the natural resources of the land along the journey.

Using Geography Themes (Bk 1 and CE, p. 127)
1. in rivers **2.** built dams to hold back water in rivers and then dug deep into the ground where water had been; dug tunnels; used huge amounts of water to break open mountain walls **3.** because the rivers became dirty when dirt and rocks were dumped there **4.** The miners had less to eat. **5.** because the rivers spread lots of rocks over farmland, so farmers could not grow enough food **6.** by selling wood from forests

Using What You've Learned

Finish the Sentence (Bk 1 and CE, p. 128)
1. 1840s **2.** Independence **3.** Canada **4.** farmland **5.** James Marshall **6.** gold **(CE) 7.** 1850

Categories (Bk 1 and CE, p. 128)
1. Gold Rush **2.** James Beckwourth **3.** Oregon Trail **4.** California

Reading a Historical Map (Bk 1 and CE, p. 129)
1. the 13 Colonies **2.** Florida **3.** Oregon Country **4.** Mexican Cession **5.** Gadsden Purchase

45

COMPLETE
EDITION

CHAPTER 20

THE SOUTHERN STATES LEAVE

BOOK 1

CHAPTER 20

TEACHING STRATEGIES

Summary: The North and the South disagreed over slavery. In 1861 the South started a country called the Confederate States of America.

Objective: Students will understand the reasons the South left the United States in 1861.

Pre-Reading Activities: 1. Have students describe the pictures on pages 130 and 131. Explain that slavery caused families to be separated if they were sold to different owners. 2. Ask students how people today protest different issues. Suggest things like books, newspapers, speeches, rallies, etc. Tell how some of these same methods were used to protest slavery in the 1800s.

Vocabulary Activities: Have students look at the pictures in the chapter to write sentences that include the new vocabulary words.

Review Words: slavery, nation, tobacco, crops, Constitution, cotton, abolitionists, Congress

Post-Reading Discussion Points: 1. Ask students why farmers in the North and the South disagreed over whether slaves were needed to help grow crops. 2. Have students discuss the meaning of the statement "a slave is not free." 3. Have students discuss why many ex-slaves like Harriet Tubman risked their lives to help other slaves escape from the South.

ELL Activity: Explain to students that President Lincoln worked to change something he believed was wrong. Ask students to think of others that worked to change something they believed was wrong. The person can be from history or from the student's own life. Have each student write about this person, and what he or she changed.

Geography Theme Activities: 1. Help students determine the region of the United States in which they live. Have them identify how places in their region are alike. 2. Have students write *The South* in the center of the Concept Web graphic organizer on page 109 of this guide. Then have them use the spokes to list how the southern states were alike. Have students make a Concept Web for the North.

Follow-Up Activities: 1. Have students report on the Underground Railroad, Harriet Tubman, Frederick Douglass, or Harriet Beecher Stowe. 2. Have students write a paragraph describing differences between the North and the South.

Chapter Online Resources:
Find more information about topics in this chapter at *www.HarcourtAchieve.com/AchievementZone.* Click on *America's Story.*

ANSWER KEY

Learning from Pictures: slaves; picking cotton

Using Geography Themes (Bk 1 and CE, p. 135)
1. It had good soil, rain, and a warm climate during most of the year. 2. cotton 3. The South did not have many big cities, factories, and railroads; most people in the South worked at farming. 4. They wanted to keep their slaves and their way of life. 5. Delaware, Kentucky, Maryland, and West Virginia

Using What You've Learned

True or False (Bk 1 and CE, p. 136)
1. T 2. T 3. F 4. F 5. F 6. T 7. F 8. T

Fact or Opinion (Bk 1 and CE, p. 136)
1. F 2. O 3. F 4. O 5. F 6. O 7. F 8. O 9. F

Reading a Bar Graph (Bk 1 and CE, p. 137)
1. 22 million 2. 3 1/2 million 3. Northerners
4. Free Southerners 5. 9 1/2 million

Journal Writing (Bk 1 and CE, p. 137)
Answers will vary. Paragraphs should identify Harriet Tubman as a slave who escaped, only to return to the South and help other slaves escape to Canada. Students might say that Harriet Tubman wanted other slaves to be free or that slaves were not treated well in the South.

TEACHING STRATEGIES

Summary: The Civil War began in 1861. The South surrendered in 1865 and rejoined the United States. The slaves were freed.

Objective: Students will understand that the United States remained one nation because the North won the Civil War.

Pre-Reading Activities: 1. Have students use the map on page 139 to name the eleven Confederate States. Ask students if their state was part of the Union, part of the Confederate States, or not yet a state. 2. Ask students what the pictures on pages 138 and 140 tell them about the way the Civil War was fought.

Vocabulary Activities: Call on students to use each word correctly in a sentence.

Review Words: Union, fort, plantations, capital, surrendered, general, slavery, nation, captured, manage

Post-Reading Discussion Points: 1. Ask students how African American soldiers might have felt fighting for the Union against Confederate soldiers. Explain to students that if African American soldiers were captured, they were enslaved. 2. Have students discuss whether they would be willing to fight against their family or friends for something in which they believed.

Primary Source Quote: Abraham Lincoln wrote these words in a letter to Horace Greeley who had publicly accused Lincoln of being pro-slavery.

ELL Activity: Explain to students that the Emancipation Proclamation improved life for all African Americans in the United States. Have students research other laws that have improved life for Americans.

Follow-Up Activities: 1. Ask students to use the Geography Theme: Region blackline master on page 120 of this guide to describe the North or the South. Tell students to use the map on page 139 or any outside resources to complete this activity.

Chapter Online Resources:
Find more information about topics in this chapter at *www.HarcourtAchieve.com/AchievementZone.* Click on *America's Story.*

ANSWER KEY

Using Maps (Bk 1 and CE, p. 139)
Most free states were located in the North. There were also two states in the West.

Learning from Pictures (Bk 1 and CE, p. 141)
he was shot

Using What You've Learned

Write the Answer (Bk 1 and CE, p. 142)
1. The North fought so that all states would remain in the Union. 2. The South fought to have its own country, the Confederate States of America. 3. The Emancipation Proclamation said all slaves in the Confederate states were free. 4. Women helped by caring for soldiers, taking care of farms and factories, and becoming spies. 5. Clara Barton was a Union nurse who cared for soldiers who were hurt in battle. **(CE) 6.** Students should identify one of the following reasons: Lee knew the Confederates could not win the war. They had little food, not enough guns, and Lee did not want more people to die. **(CE) 7.** About 600,000 soldiers died in the Civil War. **(CE) 8.** President Lincoln wanted Americans to work together to rebuild the South and for people in the North and the South to like one another again. **(CE) 9.** President Lincoln was shot five days after the Civil War ended.

Match Up (Bk 1 and CE, p. 142)
1. d 2. c 3. e 4. a 5. b

Sequencing Events (Bk 1 and CE, p. 143)
The sentences should be in the following order:
(Bk 1) 2, 1, 5, 4, 3. **(CE) 1.** In 1861 Confederate soldiers attacked Fort Sumter. 2. In 1862 President Lincoln wrote the Emancipation Proclamation. 3. In 1865 the Union captured the Confederate capital at Richmond, Virginia. 4. The war ended when General Robert E. Lee surrendered to General Ulysses S. Grant. 5. President Lincoln was killed after the war ended.

Drawing Conclusions (Bk 1 and CE, p. 143)
1. c 2. d 3. b 4. a

Journal Writing (Bk 1 and CE, p. 143)
Answers will vary. Sentences should either describe the battle at Fort Sumter or the capture of Richmond and Lee's surrender. Students may also mention the causes or results of the Civil War.

Reading a Table (Bk 1 and CE, p. 144)
1. 9,000 2. 111,000 3. less 4. more 5. more
6. stronger than

Name _____

◁ UNIT REVIEW ▷

THE NATION GROWS AND DIVIDES

Choose the Answer   Use the time line from the unit opener to answer the questions below. Draw a circle around the correct answer.

1. When did Stephen F. Austin start an American colony in Texas?
   1821   1836   1845

2. When did California become a state?
   1845   1850   1859

3. Which event happened after Abraham Lincoln became President?
   Texas became a state.
   The United States won the Mexican War.
   The Civil War ended.

4. When was a treaty signed about Oregon?
   1836   1843   1846

5. Which land won its independence from Mexico in 1836?
   Oregon   Texas   California

Match Up   Finish each sentence in Group A with words from Group B. Write the letter of the correct answer on the blank line.

Group A

1. The Oregon Trail started in
   _____ .

2. _____ was president of Mexico during the Texas Revolution.

3. _____ helped slaves escape to Canada.

4. The border between Mexico and Texas is now the _____ .

5. _____ cared for hurt soldiers during the Civil War.

Group B

a. Rio Grande

b. Clara Barton

c. Antonio López de Santa Anna

d. Independence, Missouri

e. Harriet Tubman

© Steck-Vaughn Company

Name _____

◄ UNIT REVIEW ►
THE NATION GROWS AND DIVIDES

Riddle Review   Use a word in dark print to complete each sentence below.
Write the word on the blanks next to each sentence.

Richmond	property	Mexico	Abraham
Confederate	Cession	James	Alamo

1. After the Mexican War, it became easier for American women to own _____ .

   __ ☐ __ __ __ __ __ __

2. The Southern states called their new country the _____ States of America.

   __ __ __ __ ☐ __ __ __ __ __

3. _____ Beckwourth found a pass through the mountains.

   __ __ ☐ __ __

4. In 1846 a war started between the United States and _____ .

   __ ☐ __ __ __ __

5. Antonio López de Santa Anna won the Battle of the _____ .

   __ __ __ ☐ __

6. _____ Lincoln was President during the Civil War.

   __ ☐ __ __ __ __ __

7. After the Mexican War, Mexico sold the Mexican _____ to the United States.

   __ ☐ __ __ __ __ __

8. In 1865 Union soldiers captured _____ .

   ☐ __ __ __ __ __ __ __

The letters in the boxes spell a word. The word answers the riddle.

RIDDLE: What must students do on a test that is also what Texans said at the San Jacinto River?

ANSWER: __ __ __ __ __ __ __ __ __

Name _____

◀ UNIT TEST ▶

THE NATION GROWS AND DIVIDES

True or False Write **T** next to each sentence that is true. Write **F** next to each sentence that is false.

_____ 1. Texans did not like the Mexican laws.

_____ 2. Many people rushed to Oregon to find gold.

_____ 3. Mexico won the Mexican War against the United States.

_____ 4. The North wanted slaves to work on plantations in the West.

_____ 5. Abraham Lincoln was President of the United States during the Civil War.

_____ 6. Harriet Tubman helped many slaves escape to Canada.

Match Up Finish each sentence in Group A with words from Group B. Write the letter of the correct answer on the blank line.

Group A

1. _____ was the commander in chief of the Texan army and the first president of the Republic of Texas.

2. The leader of the Confederate army was _____ .

3. The paper that said all slaves in the Confederate states were free was the _____ .

4. Covered wagons traveled to Oregon on the _____ .

5. Americans bought the _____ to build a railroad.

Group B

a. Oregon Trail

b. Gadsden Purchase

c. Sam Houston

d. Emancipation Proclamation

e. Robert E. Lee

Name _____

◁ UNIT TEST ▷

THE NATION GROWS AND DIVIDES

Sequencing Events   Write the numbers **1, 2, 3, 4,** and **5** next to these sentences to show the correct order.

_____ The South returned to the United States after the end of the Civil War.

_____ Texas became a republic in 1836 after Santa Anna surrendered to Sam Houston.

_____ Stephen F. Austin started a colony for Americans in Texas in 1821.

_____ The United States won the Mexican War after Texas became a state.

_____ California became a state in 1850.

Finish the Sentence   Draw a circle around the word or words that finish each sentence.

1. The idea that the United States should rule land from the Atlantic Ocean to the Pacific Ocean is known as _____ .
   Manifest Destiny   Mexican Cession   the Fugitive Slave Act

2. Mexican law allowed women to _____ .
   use slaves on their farms   speak English   own property

3. The trip to Oregon on the Oregon Trail took about _____ .
   one month   six months   two years

4. The man who found a mountain pass to help settlers reach California was _____ .
   James Beckwourth   Stephen F. Austin   Ulysses S. Grant

5. In the 1800s, there were many factories in the _____ .
   West   South   North

6. Another name for the United States is the _____ .
   Confederate States of America   Congress   Union

Name _____

◄ TIME LINE REVIEW ►
AMERICA'S STORY: TO 1865

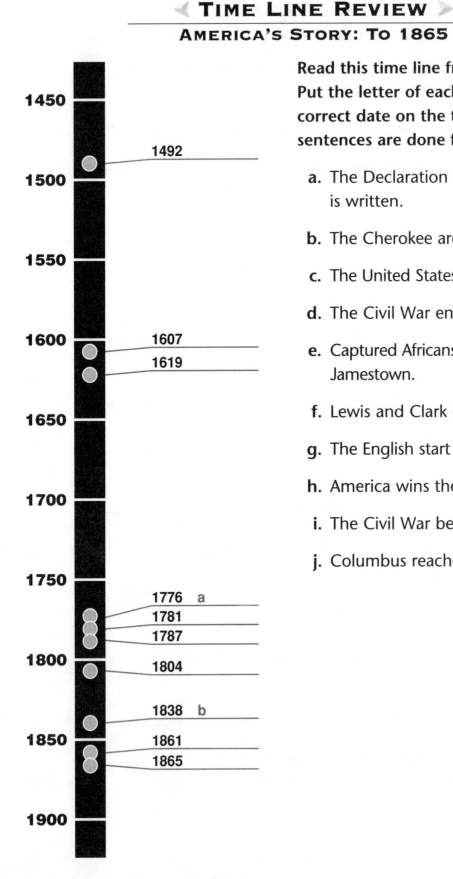

1450	
	1492
1500	
1550	
1600	1607
	1619
1650	
1700	
1750	
	1776 a
	1781
	1787
1800	1804
	1838 b
1850	1861
	1865
1900	

Read this time line from top to bottom. Put the letter of each sentence next to the correct date on the time line. The first two sentences are done for you.

a. The Declaration of Independence is written.

b. The Cherokee are forced to move west.

c. The United States Constitution is written.

d. The Civil War ends.

e. Captured Africans are brought to Jamestown.

f. Lewis and Clark explore Louisiana.

g. The English start a colony in Jamestown.

h. America wins the American Revolution.

i. The Civil War begins.

j. Columbus reaches America.

Name _____

◁ FINAL TEST ▷

AMERICA'S STORY: TO 1865

True or False   Write **T** next to each sentence that is true. Write **F** next to each sentence that is false.

_____ 1. The Spanish came to America in the 1500s to build factories.

_____ 2. The United States signed a treaty with Great Britain about Oregon.

_____ 3. The first people to live in America were the English.

_____ 4. One reason the Civil War was fought was the South wanted to have slaves.

_____ 5. One reason the French came to America was to find furs.

_____ 6. France sold Louisiana and Philadelphia to the United States in 1803.

Match Up   Finish each sentence in Group A with words from Group B. Write the letter of the correct answer on the blank line.

Group A

1. The _____ colony was started by Quakers.

2. President James K. Polk believed in _____ .

3. Emma Willard and Mary Lyon started schools for _____ .

4. Christopher Columbus wanted to find a short cut to _____ .

5. _____ asked the French people to help the United States during the American Revolution.

Group B

a. Benjamin Franklin

b. Asia

c. Pennsylvania

d. Manifest Destiny

e. girls

Name _____

◁ FINAL TEST ▷

AMERICA'S STORY: TO 1865

Sequencing Events   Write the numbers **1, 2, 3, 4,** and **5** next to these sentences to show the correct order.

_____ The Mexican War was fought after Texas became a state.

_____ Americans fought against Great Britain in the War of 1812.

_____ The Pilgrims had their first Thanksgiving.

_____ The Civil War began between the Union and the Confederate States.

_____ Americans fought for their freedom from Great Britain in the American Revolution.

Finish the Sentence   Draw a circle around the word or words that finish each sentence.

1. The Constitution allows Americans to _____ .
   vote for their President, senators, and representatives
   choose a new person to be king
   help write laws in Parliament

2. _____ was the first President of the United States and helped write the Constitution.
   William Clark   George Washington   James K. Polk

3. Andrew Jackson forced Native Americans to move _____ .
   west of the Mississippi River   to Oregon   to Florida

4. Americans wrote the _____ to say that the American colonies were free.
   Mayflower Compact   Declaration of Independence   Constitution

5. The states in the Confederate States of America were from the _____ .
   North   South   West

6. The _____ was a change from making goods by hand to making them by machine.
   Industrial Revolution   Constitutional Convention   Mexican Cession

TEACHING STRATEGIES

Summary: After the Civil War, Americans began to rebuild the United States into a strong, growing nation. Railroads and inventions made life easier in America.

Major Concepts:
- **Geography:** The Homestead Act helped settle the West. Imperialism led to the gaining of Alaska, Hawaii, Guam, and Puerto Rico.
- **History:** The Spanish-American War was fought to help Cuba become free from Spain.
- **Sociology:** African Americans gained rights. Segregation laws were introduced. Native Americans were moved to reservations. Railroads and inventions made life easier.

Pre-Reading Activities: **1.** Explain that most African Americans at this time had been born and raised in slavery. Ask students what kinds of problems African Americans might have had starting new lives after slavery. **2.** Help students use a political map to locate territories of the United States. Ask students why there are American territories so far from the continental United States. **3.** Have students look at the time line in the unit opener. Ask them to calculate about how many years of American history this unit covers. Then ask them to predict the main ideas of the unit based on the information in the unit time line, the title of the unit, and the picture in the unit opener.

Post-Reading Discussion Points: **1.** Ask students to explain some of the difficulties African Americans and Native Americans faced after the Civil War. **2.** Have students describe how the size of the United States and its relationship with other nations was affected by imperialism. **3.** Call on students to describe ways that inventions make life in America better.

Follow-Up Activities: **1.** Help students use the Concept Web graphic organizer on page 109 of this guide. In the center have students write *The United States changed after the Civil War.* Students should write supporting facts on the spokes. **2.** Ask students to discuss ways the United States could have better handled the settlement of Native American lands in the 1800s.

Review Activities: Refer to pages 60–61 of this guide for review activities for this unit.

Assessment: Refer to pages 62–63 of this guide for the Unit Test.

ANSWER KEY

Unit Review (Bk 2, p. 29; CE, p. 173)

1. Reconstruction **2.** slaves **3.** Homestead Act **4.** Great Plains **5.** reservations **6.** imperialism **7.** Alaska **8.** Hawaii **9.** Edison

Unit Review (Teacher's Guide, pp. 60–61)

Choose the Answer **1.** 1869 **2.** 1898 **3.** 1876 **4.** Alaska

Match Up **1.** d **2.** a **3.** c **4.** b **5.** e

Riddle Review **1.** buffalo **2.** African **3.** Cuba **4.** elevators **5.** horses **6.** farmers **7.** buy
Answer: F A C T O R Y

Unit Test (Teacher's Guide, pp. 62–63)

True or False **1.** T **2.** T **3.** F **4.** T **5.** F **6.** T

Match Up **1.** d **2.** e **3.** a **4.** b **5.** c

Sequencing Events The sentences should be numbered 4, 3, 1, 2, 5.

Finish the Sentence **1.** rules **2.** Native Americans **3.** railroad **4.** make shoes quickly **5.** Garrett Morgan **6.** Guam

TEACHING STRATEGIES

Summary: The South had to be rebuilt after the Civil War. Education and laws helped African Americans after slavery was ended.

Objective: Students will understand the changes in America during the Reconstruction period.

Pre-Reading Activities: **1.** Have students look at the map in this chapter. Help students make a time line showing the states and the dates they rejoined the Union. **2.** Ask students what it might have been like to be slaves who were suddenly set free without homes or jobs. Then, have them consider how they might have felt if they had been plantation owners who were used to having slaves work without being paid.

Vocabulary Activities: **1.** Have students list words from the chapter that begin with the prefix *re-* (*rejoined* and *Reconstruction*). Ask students to tell what the prefix *re-* means. **2.** Have students use the vocabulary words in oral sentences.

Review Words
(Bk 1 and CE, Chaps. 1–21) Civil War, destroyed, rebuild, plantations, cotton, slavery, senators, representatives, Congress, Constitution, amendments

Post-Reading Discussion Points: **1.** Ask students why it was more difficult for the South than the North to recover from the war. **2.** Ask students to imagine how the first African American senators and representatives might have felt in Congress. Would they feel proud, honored, or nervous?

Primary Source Quote: Booker T. Washington wrote these words in his autobiography *Up From Slavery.*

ELL Activity: The Fifteenth Amendment allowed African American men to vote. Have students write a paragraph about what it might have been like for African American men to vote for the first time.

Primary Source Activities: **1.** Have students read the Thirteenth, Fourteenth, and Fifteenth amendments of the Constitution. Discuss the main ideas of each amendment. **2.** Read and discuss other excerpts from Booker T. Washington's book *Up From Slavery.*

Follow-Up Activities: **1.** Have students read and report on Booker T. Washington and the Tuskegee Institute.

Chapter Online Resources:
Find more information about topics in this chapter at *www.HarcourtAchieve.com/AchievementZone.* Click on *America's Story.*

ANSWER KEY

Learning from Pictures (Bk 2, p. 4; CE, p. 148)
Possible Answers: happy, thankful, excited, relieved

Using Maps (Bk 2, p. 5; CE p. 149)
Mississippi and Texas

Using Primary Sources (Bk 2, p. 7; CE, p. 151)
1. by walking and begging rides in wagons and cars **2.** about 82 miles **3.** upon the ground **4.** fifty cents **5. Constructed Response** Answers will vary. Washington was eager to get an education.

Using What You've Learned

Finish the Story (Bk 2, p. 8; CE, p. 152)
1. Reconstruction **2.** rebuilt **3.** slavery **4.** equal rights **5.** vote **6.** fair

Using Graphic Organizers: Main Idea and Supporting Details
1. African Americans had many problems after they became free. **2.** Booker T. Washington helped African Americans get better jobs.

TEACHING STRATEGIES

Summary: The Homestead Act and railroads helped Americans settle the West. Native Americans were forced to move to reservations.

Objective: Students will understand why many Americans settled in the West and how this settlement affected Native Americans.

Pre-Reading Activities: 1. Have students look at the pictures in this chapter. Ask them how they would feel about moving to the Great Plains as it is depicted in these photos. **2.** Ask students how and why the United States might have encouraged people to move to new areas of the country.

Vocabulary Activities: 1. Have students use a dictionary to find at least three meanings of the word *reservation*. Discuss how the word is used in this chapter. **2.** Call on students to use each vocabulary word in a sentence.

Review Words
(Bk 1 and CE, Chaps. 1–21) senators, representatives, Congress, settlers, Civil War, buffalo, gold rush, miners, crops

Post-Reading Discussion Points: 1. Discuss why the settlement of the Great Plains was slow and why the railroad became important. **2.** Ask students why the United States gave settlers free land on the Great Plains. **3.** Ask why settlers wanted Native Americans to live in one place. Then ask why Native Americans did not want to live on reservations.

Primary Source Quote: Sidney Dillon, a Union Pacific official, is recalling in 1892 the great accomplishments of the transcontinental railroad.

ELL Activity: The railroad changed the lives of all Americans. Have students label on a map places where the railroad made stops. Have students pick one location. Ask them to use the internet to learn more about the location.

Geography Theme Activities: 1. Have students research and report on another region of the United States. **2.** Read to the students the chapter "Grasshoppers Walking" from *On the Banks of Plum Creek* by Laura Ingalls Wilder. Discuss Wilder's description of the grasshopper invasion of the Great Plains.

Follow-Up Activities: 1. Have students study people who helped build the transcontinental railroad. **2.** Help students use the Cause and Effect graphic organizer on page 111 of this guide to show how the West became settled.

Chapter Online Resources:
Find more information about topics in this chapter at *www.HarcourtAchieve.com/AchievementZone.* Click on *America's Story.*

ANSWER KEY

Learning from Pictures (Bk 2, p. 9; CE, p. 153)
Answers will vary. Students may mention that there were no neighbors nearby, there were no stores, they had to grow their own food, build their own home, and make their own clothes.

Using Maps (Bk 2, p. 11; CE, p. 155)
Great Plains

Using Geography Themes (Bk 2, p. 14; CE, p. 158)
1. dry, flat land with few trees; tall and short grasses; hard, grass-covered land **2.** with sod cut into large blocks that were stacked to make houses **3.** There were hot and dry summers; winters had terrible snowstorms; there were dangerous windstorms. **4.** because it grows wheat, corn, and other grains for the United States and other nations **5.** North Dakota, South Dakota, Nebraska, and Kansas

Using What You've Learned

Match Up (Bk 2, p. 15; CE, p. 159)
1. d **2.** a **3.** c **4.** b **5.** e

Cause and Effect (Bk 2, p. 15; CE, p. 159)
1. b **2.** d **3.** a **4.** c **(CE) 5.** e

Reading a Flow Chart (Bk 2, p. 16; CE, p. 160)
1. grow **2.** kernels **3.** vitamins **4.** bags

Journal Writing (Bk 2, p. 16; CE, p. 160)
Answers will vary. Students may mention great distances, loneliness, little rain, harsh winters, windstorms, snowstorms, danger from Native Americans, dificulty growing food, or crops eaten by insects.

TEACHING STRATEGIES

Summary: Imperialism and the Spanish-American War helped the United States gain new territories such as Alaska, Hawaii, Guam, and Puerto Rico. The war freed Cuba and other nations from Spain.

Objective: Students will understand the reasons for the Spanish-American war and how the idea of imperialism led to growth for the United States.

Pre-Reading Activities: **1.** Have students look at the map in this chapter. Have them locate Alaska, the Hawaiian Islands, Cuba, Puerto Rico, Guam, and the Philippines. **2.** Have students look at the pictures of Alaska and Hawaii in this chapter. Ask them to give reasons why the United States might have wanted Alaska and Hawaii to become states.

Vocabulary Activities: Help students explain the meaning of each vocabulary word. Have students explain how they think these words might be used in the chapter.

Review Words
(Bk 1 and CE, Chaps. 1–21) plantations, citizens, gold rush, sugar cane, captured, nation, surrendered, independent, Civil War, Congress, republic, colony

Post-Reading Discussion Points: **1.** Ask students to explain some of the reasons that Americans wanted Alaska and Hawaii to become states. **2.** Ask students why Americans might have wanted to help Cuba fight for independence from Spain. Remind them that Americans fought for freedom in the American Revolution. **3.** Ask students to compare the ideas of imperialism and Manifest Destiny. Have them list lands that the United States obtained using each idea.

Primary Source Quote: Queen Liliuokalani wrote an autobiography in 1898. She died in 1917.

ELL Activity: The United States bought Alaska from Russia in 1867. Have students work in groups to create a presentation about Alaska. It may be about its history, native peoples, or current events. Have students present to the class.

Follow-Up Activities: **1.** Help students use the Sequencing graphic organizer on page 110 of this guide to show how the United States gained new territory in the late 1800s. **2.** Have students use the Geography Theme: Region blackline master on page 120 of this guide to describe the different regions of one of the new lands gained by the United States in the late 1800s. Give students a map of the chosen state or territory and other resources to help them complete this activity.

Chapter Online Resources:
Find more information about topics in this chapter at *www.HarcourtAchieve.com/AchievementZone.* Click on *America's Story.*

ANSWER KEY

Learning from Pictures (Bk 2, p. 17; CE, p. 161)
trees, land, and water

Using Maps (Bk 2, p. 18; CE, p. 162)
Hawaiian Islands and Guam

Using What You've Learned

Choose the Answer (Bk 2, p. 21; CE, p. 165)
1. imperialism **2.** Russia **3.** gold **4.** 1959 **5.** Cuba
6. a battleship **7.** Spain **8.** the Philippines
9. Guam and Puerto Rico

Fact or Opinion (Bk 2, pp. 21–22; CE, pp. 165–166)
1. F **2.** O **3.** F **4.** F **5.** O **6.** F **(CE) 7.** O
(CE) 8. F

Sequencing Events (CE, p. 166)
The sentences should be in the following order:
1. In 1867 the United States bought Alaska.
2. Hawaii became a republic in 1894. **3.** Many Americans were killed when the *Maine* blew up.
4. The Spanish-American War began and ended.
5. Alaska became the forty-ninth state in 1959.

Using Map Directions (Bk 2, p. 22; CE, p. 166)
1. Alaska **2.** west **3.** Cuba **4.** northwest
5. southeast

Journal Writing (Bk 2, p. 22; CE, p. 166)
Paragraphs will vary. Paragraphs might say that Alaska is large and has gold, furs, good fishing, and oil.

TEACHING STRATEGIES

Summary: Inventions such as the telephone, light bulb, elevator, automobile, and airplane have dramatically changed the way Americans live.

Objective: Students will learn about different inventors and understand how inventions have helped make life better for Americans.

Pre-Reading Activities: 1. Ask students if they know when the telephone, the electric light bulb, or the automobile was invented. **2.** Have students write *Important Inventions* in the center of the Concept Web graphic organizer on page 109 of this guide. Ask students to list on the spokes the inventions they feel have been most important in their own lives. Have students compare their webs. **3.** Invite an older citizen to speak to the class about what America was like before automobiles, computers, or television.

Vocabulary Activities: Call out a new word to the class. Then ask a student to think of a word that relates to the new word. Have the next student say a word that relates to the previous student's word. Continue with each student until all students have participated. Start over with another word from the vocabulary list.

Review Words
(Bk 2, Chaps. 1–3; CE, Chaps. 22–24) immigrants
(Bk 1 and CE, Chaps. 1–21) invented

Post-Reading Discussion Points: 1. Ask students to explain which of the inventions discussed in this chapter are most important to them. **2.** Ask students why it is important for people to keep finding new ways to improve life. Suggest that they try to imagine a world without wheels, medicine, or tools.

Primary Source Quote: Orville Wright explains in his own words about the first flight in the world.

ELL Activity: Have students pick one inventor from the chapter and write a short biography about the person's life and contributions to technology.

Follow-Up Activities: 1. Have students report on different inventors, such as George Washington Carver, Robert Fulton, Eli Whitney, or an inventor discussed in the chapter. **2.** List different inventions on the side of the Feature Chart graphic organizer on page 113 of this guide. Across the top write different areas that inventions might affect, such as communication, travel, homes, or factories. Help students use the analysis to write a short paper on the importance of inventions. **3.** Ask students to research the origin of the phrase, "the real McCoy" based on the African American inventor, Elijah McCoy. **4.** Have students work in groups to list any things they might like to invent to make their own lives easier.

Chapter Online Resources:
Find more information about topics in this chapter at *www.HarcourtAchieve.com/AchievementZone*. Click on *America's Story*.

ANSWER KEY

Learning from Pictures:
Answers will vary, but should include a description of how planes look today, how fast they can travel, and how many passengers they can carry.

Using What You've Learned

Choose a Word (Bk 2, p. 27; CE, p. 171)
1. invention **2.** telephone **3.** Edison
4. shoes **5.** skyscraper **6.** Wright

Using Graphic Organizers: Sequencing Events
(Bk 2, p. 27; CE, p. 171)
4, 1, 3, 2

Reading a Chart (Bk 2, p. 28; CE, p. 172)
1. top to bottom **2.** left to right **3.** Henry Ford
4. airplane **(CE) 5.** Garrett Morgan

Name _____

‹ UNIT REVIEW ›

AFTER THE CIVIL WAR

Choose the Answer Use the time line from the unit opener to answer the questions below. Draw a circle around the correct answer.

1. When was the first railroad that went across the United States finished?
   1865   1869   1882

2. Hawaii became part of the United States and the United States won the Spanish-American War in which year?
   1862   1879   1898

3. Alexander Graham Bell invented the telephone in which year?
   1865   1876   1896

4. Which land did the United States buy in 1867?
   Hawaii   Spain   Alaska

Match Up Finish each sentence in Group A with words from Group B. Write the letter of the correct answer on the blank line.

Group A

1. In the Spanish-American War, American soldiers fought to help _____ become free.

2. Thousands of _____ people helped build the railroads across the United States.

3. _____ started a school for African Americans called the Tuskegee Institute.

4. The Thirteenth Amendment ended _____ in the United States.

5. _____ proved that people could fly in airplanes.

Group B

a. Chinese

b. slavery

c. Booker T. Washington

d. Cuba

e. Orville and Wilbur Wright

Name _____

◄ UNIT REVIEW ►
AFTER THE CIVIL WAR

Riddle Review   Use a word in dark print to complete each sentence below. Write the word on the blanks next to each sentence.

buy	African	farmers	elevators
Cuba	buffalo	horses	

1. Native Americans hunted _____ on the Great Plains.

___ ___ □ ___ ___ ___

2. The Fifteenth Amendment to the Constitution said _____ American men could vote.

___ ___ ___ ___ ___ □ ___

3. Puerto Rico and _____ belonged to Spain before the Spanish-American War.

□ ___ ___ ___

4. Skyscrapers use _____ to move people from floor to floor.

___ ___ ___ ___ ___ □ ___ ___

5. Before there were cars, people traveled in wagons or on _____ .

___ □ ___ ___ ___ ___

6. Many Americans moved to the Great Plains and became _____ .

___ ___ □ ___ ___ ___ ___

7. In 1867 the United States decided to _____ Alaska.

___ ___ □

The letters in the boxes spell a word. The word answers the riddle.

RIDDLE: Where can a car move even when its engine is turned off?

ANSWER: ___ ___ ___ ___ ___ ___ ___

Name _____

◁ UNIT TEST ▷

AFTER THE CIVIL WAR

True or False   Write **T** next to each sentence that is true. Write **F** next to each sentence that is false.

_____ 1. After the Civil War, the South had to rebuild its roads, farms, and cities.

_____ 2. The United States government forced Native Americans on the Great Plains to move to reservations.

_____ 3. People living in Cuba today are United States citizens.

_____ 4. Henry Ford made one of the first cars in the United States.

_____ 5. Immigrants were not allowed to help build railroads in the United States.

_____ 6. Booker T. Washington helped African Americans get better jobs.

Match Up   Finish each sentence in Group A with words from Group B. Write the letter of the correct answer on the blank line.

Group A

1. The law in the Constitution that ended slavery was the _____ .

2. The idea that African Americans could not sit in train cars with white people is _____ .

3. The idea that one country should rule other countries or colonies is _____ .

4. Henry Ford invented the _____ .

5. Alaska had gold and _____ .

Group B

a. imperialism

b. assembly line

c. oil

d. Thirteenth Amendment

e. segregation

Name _____

◀ UNIT TEST ▶

AFTER THE CIVIL WAR

Sequencing Events   Write the numbers **1**, **2**, **3**, **4**, and **5** next to these sentences to show the correct order.

_____   Gold was found in Alaska in 1896.

_____   Thomas Edison invented the electric light bulb in 1879.

_____   In 1862 the Homestead Act was written to help people settle in the West.

_____   The North won the Civil War.

_____   The United States battleship called the *Maine* blew up near Cuba.

Finish the Sentence   Draw a circle around the word or words that finish each sentence.

1. Under the idea called imperialism, one country _____ another country.
   rules   trades with   fights

2. Many _____ made tools and weapons from buffalo horns and bones.
   Cuban soldiers   Native Americans   farmers on the Great Plains

3. The fastest way to travel across the West was on a _____ .
   railroad   horse   covered wagon

4. Jan Matzeliger invented a machine to _____ .
   make cars quickly   make shoes quickly   make airplanes quickly

5. The traffic light was invented by _____ .
   Garrett Morgan   Thomas Edison   Henry Ford

6. Puerto Rico and _____ are part of the United States.
   Cuba   Guam   the Philippines

TEACHING STRATEGIES

Summary: The United States changed rapidly in the late 1800s and early 1900s as a result of immigrants coming to America and the growth of businesses and labor unions. With these changes came problems, which many Americans worked to solve.

Major Concepts:
- **Geography:** The movement of immigrants to the United States greatly increased the population.
- **Government:** Conflicts between big business and labor led to new laws designed to protect American workers.
- **Sociology:** As millions of immigrants arrived, American culture changed. The immigrants often lived and worked in very crowded conditions. Reformers worked to improve life for Americans.

Pre-Reading Activities: 1. Ask students how they think the addition of immigrants from so many different nations affected America. 2. Ask students what large businesses can be found in their community. How do these businesses affect life in the community? 3. Have students look at the time line in the unit opener. Ask them to calculate about how many years of American history this unit covers. Then ask them to predict the main ideas of the unit based on the information in the unit time line, the title of the unit, and the picture in the unit opener.

Post-Reading Discussion Points: 1. Ask students to explain some of the problems faced by immigrants. Have them discuss some of the individuals who helped immigrants. 2. Ask students to tell how Andrew Carnegie and John D. Rockefeller owned so many businesses and made so much money. 3. Have students explain what a labor union is and how union leaders and other individuals work to improve workers' lives.

Follow-Up Activities: 1. Have students debate whether it is fair for a few companies to control many businesses. 2. Encourage students to learn more about the American labor unions. How have unions helped American workers? 3. Have students use the

Event Description graphic organizer on page 114 of this guide to show important information about the United States as it became a modern nation. In the center box, have students write *The United States becomes a modern nation*. Students should complete the rest of the organizer with information from this unit.

Review Activities: Refer to pages 70–71 of this guide for review activities covering this unit.

Assessment: Refer to pages 72–73 of this guide for the Unit Test.

ANSWER KEY

Unit Review (Bk 2, p. 61; CE, p. 205)
1. immigrants 2. reporter 3. problems 4. steel 5. big business 6. oil 7. labor unions 8. Hull House 9. Lillian Wald 10. lead 11. Theodore Roosevelt 12. Upton Sinclair 13. muckrakers 14. equal rights

Unit Review (Teacher's Guide, pp. 70–71)

Choose the Answer 1. 1889 2. Susan B. Anthony 3. 1859 4. John D. Rockefeller built his first oil refinery.

Match Up 1. c 2. d 3. e 4. a 5. b

Riddle Review 1. railroads 2. Hine 3. Barrett 4. Pure 5. millionaire 6. slaves 7. Jones 8. Tarbell
Answer: A I R P L A N E

Unit Test (Teacher's Guide, pp. 72–73)

True or False 1. T 2. T 3. T 4. F 5. T 6. T

Match Up 1. b 2. a 3. e 4. d 5. c

Sequencing Events The sentences should be numbered 2, 4, 5, 3, 1.

Finish the Sentence 1. steel mills 2. Lewis Hine 3. Upton Sinclair 4. African Americans 5. unions 6. Samuel Gompers

TEACHING STRATEGIES

Summary: Immigrants have come to America from many countries and for many reasons. Immigrants have helped build America.

Objective: Students will understand the origins, problems, and contributions of immigrants to the United States.

Pre-Reading Activities: 1. Have a recent immigrant to the United States speak to the class about his or her reasons for coming to the United States. **2.** Conduct a poll of the class to find out the original countries of each student's ancestors. Help students use the Concept Web graphic organizer on page 109 of this guide to show all the different countries listed. Write *Ancestors' Original Countries* in the center of the web. Then write the names of the countries on the spokes.

Vocabulary Activities: Discuss the meaning of *reporter.* Invite students to name ways a reporter might gather information about a topic.

Review Words
(Bk 2, Chaps. 1–4; CE, Chaps. 22–25) immigrants (Bk 1 and CE, Chaps. 1–21) freedom of religion, slavery, Civil War, citizens, gold rush, miners

Post-Reading Discussion Points: 1. Discuss the different reasons immigrants came to the United States. **2.** Discuss the difficulties immigrants had when they arrived. Emphasize cultural and language differences. **3.** Discuss how the immigration of African Americans was different from that of other groups.

Primary Source Quote: This quote is from a letter written by Josephine Roche on July 10, 1893, to her mother, who was living in Athens, Greece

ELL Activity: Have students collect oral histories from relatives about how and why their family came to the United States.

Geography Theme Activities 1. On a political map of the United States, have students identify other harbor cities on the Atlantic Ocean, such as Charleston and Boston. **2.** Have students choose a United States city to research and write about.

Follow-Up Activities: 1. Have students research and report on what it was like to be an immigrant in the 1800s. **2.** Have students research why Ellis Island and the Statue of Liberty were important to immigrants. **3.** Have students bring ethnic foods from home to share with the class.

Chapter Online Resources:
Find more information about topics in this chapter at *www.HarcourtAchieve.com/AchievementZone.* Click on *America's Story.*

ANSWER KEY

Learning from Pictures (Bk 2, p. 32; CE, p. 176)
Answers will vary, but students may include that immigrants might have felt nervous, excited, afraid, or full of hope when they arrived from Europe.

Using Maps (Bk 2, p. 34; CE, p. 178)
Students should list two of the following: Great Britain, Ireland, Germany, or Italy.

Using Geography Themes (Bk 2, p. 36; CE, p. 180)
1. since 1790 **2.** that the United States is a land of freedom **3.** Little Italy and Chinatown **4.** Manhattan, Bronx, Queens, Staten Island, and Brooklyn **5.** the Atlantic Ocean

Using What You've Learned

Find the Answers (Bk 2, p. 37; CE, p. 181)
Students should choose the following sentences:
2. Some people wanted freedom of religion.
3. Some people did not like the laws of their own country.

Using Graphic Organizers: Concept Web
(Bk 2, p. 37; CE, p. 181)
1. Chinese Immigrants **2.** Immigrant Life
3. Jacob Riis

Journal Writing (Bk 2, p. 37; CE, p. 181)
Paragraphs will vary. Answers may include that immigrants had to learn to read, write, and speak English; they lived in small, crowded houses; they worked in dirty factories; they were paid very little; their children had to work all day in factories; there were no parks where immigrant children could play.

Reading a Bar Graph (Bk 2, p. 38; CE, p. 182)
1. Italy **2.** Japan **3.** British **4.** 100,000
5. more than **(CE) 6.** Italian

TEACHING STRATEGIES

Summary: Steel, oil, and railroads were examples of big business in the United States. Congress passed laws to keep a few companies from controlling all the big business.

Objective: Students will understand how big business grew in the United States.

Pre-Reading Activities: 1. Have students make a list of items that use steel or oil. Ask students why steel and oil are important in the United States today. **2.** Ask students which businesses might be considered big business today. Suggest the computer or electric industries.

Vocabulary Activities: 1. Write *big business, steel mills,* and *oil refineries* on the chalkboard. Call on students to define one part of each term. Then ask students to use these separate definitions to infer meanings for the complete terms. **2.** Have students write sentences using each new word.

Review Words
(Bk 2, Chaps. 1–5; CE, Chaps. 22–26) salaries, immigrants
(Bk 1 and CE, Chaps. 1–21) Civil War, nation, Congress

Post-Reading Discussion Points: 1. Have students discuss why railroads became a big business in the 1800s. Ask students how and why the railroad business has changed. **2.** Discuss why the government wanted to keep one company from controlling a single product. **3.** Ask students how Andrew Carnegie and John D. Rockefeller used their wealth to benefit others.

Primary Source Quote: Andrew Carnegie came to the United States in 1848 as a young boy with his family, who were poor. By 1890 his annual income was about $25 million.

ELL Activity: Have students invite a local businessperson to discuss how he or she got started in business. Have students prepare a list of questions to ask that would give them an understanding of what is necessary to start a business.

Follow-Up Activities: 1. Have students read about and report on the life story of Andrew Carnegie or John D. Rockefeller. **2.** Ask students to use the Feature Chart graphic organizer on page 113 of this guide to compare Andrew Carnegie and John D. Rockefeller in regard to their companies and contributions. **3.** Have students use the Geography Theme: Region blackline master on page 120 of this guide to describe natural resource and industry regions in the United States. Tell students to use the map in this chapter along with any outside references to complete this activity.

Chapter Online Resources:
Find more information about topics in this chapter at *www.HarcourtAchieve.com/AchievementZone.* Click on *America's Story.*

ANSWER KEY

Learning from Pictures (Bk 2, p. 40; CE, p. 184)
Answers will vary, but should include that the air must have been thick with smoke and it might have been hard to breathe.

Using What You've Learned

True or False (Bk 2, p. 42; CE, p. 186)
1. T **2.** F **3.** T **4.** F **5.** T **6.** T

Using Graphic Organizers: Cause and Effect
(Bk 2, p. 42; CE, p. 186)
1. d **2.** c **3.** a **4.** b

Using a Map Key to Read a Resource Map
(Bk 2, p. 43; CE, p. 187)
1. coal **2.** Students should list three of the following: Alabama, Alaska, Colorado, Illinois, Indiana, Iowa, Kansas, Kentucky, Michigan, Missouri, Montana, New Mexico, North Dakota, Ohio, Pennsylvania, Tennessee, Utah, Washington, West Virginia, Wyoming. **3.** Students should list three of the following: Alabama, California, Georgia, Idaho, Michigan, Minnesota, Missouri, Montana, Nevada, New York, Pennsylvania, Tennessee, Virginia, Washington, Wisconsin. **4.** oil **5.** iron ore
6. Students should write one of the following: Michigan, Montana, Pennsylvania. **(CE) 7.** oil

TEACHING STRATEGIES

Summary: Workers often had to work long hours in dangerous factories for low wages. Labor unions were started to help workers get better working conditions and higher pay.

Objective: Students will understand why labor unions were developed and how they helped American workers.

Pre-Reading Activities: 1. Ask students to write a paragraph describing one of the pictures in this chapter. Ask students why it might be terrible for children to work in factories. **2.** Have students identify any safety hazards, such as a lack of protective gear, that they can see in the pictures in this chapter. **3.** Ask students what they might do to get their employer to change working conditions.

Vocabulary Activities: 1. Have students play a game with the vocabulary terms. For example, give students one set of index cards with the vocabulary words and another set of index cards with definitions. Have students match the vocabulary words with the definitions. **2.** Ask students why American Federation of Labor is often shortened to AFL. Help students think of other examples of acronyms.

Review Words
(Bk 2, Chaps. 1–6; CE, Chaps. 22–27) immigrants, salaries
(Bk 1 and CE, Chaps. 1–21) published, goods, miners, Civil War

Post-Reading Discussion Points: 1. Discuss the reasons employers used child labor. Why might large families want their children to work? **2.** Discuss the purposes of labor unions. Ask students if they think labor unions are still necessary today. **3.** Discuss how photographs of young factory workers helped change people's ideas about letting children work in factories.

Primary Source Quote: Samuel Gompers is credited with organizing millions of members of various labor unions into a single organized union.

ELL Activity: Have students work in pairs to role-play a factory worker who wants to join a union and a factory worker who does not. Have them list reasons for and against joining a union.

Follow-Up Activities: 1. Have students role-play workers and management discussing a union demand for higher wages, child care, or better health insurance. **2.** Have students research and study the photographs of Lewis Hine. Ask students to show the class the photographs they found most moving. **3.** Have students research and report on the life and work of Mary "Mother" Jones or Samuel Gompers.

Chapter Online Resources:
Find more information about topics in this chapter at *www.HarcourtAchieve.com/AchievementZone*. Click on *America's Story.*

ANSWER KEY

Learning from Pictures (Bk 2, p. 45; CE, p. 189)
Answers will vary, but should include that working in a factory was often dangerous, overcrowded, tiring, and difficult.

Using What You've Learned

Finish the Sentence (Bk 2, p. 48; CE, p. 192)
1. labor unions **2.** on strike **3.** Labor
(CE) 4. photographs

Drawing Conclusions (Bk 2, p. 48; CE, p. 192)
1. b **2.** c **(CE) 3.** d **4.** a

Reading a Line Graph (Bk 2, p. 49; CE, p. 193)
1. millions **2.** 1900 **3.** 1980 **4.** 5 million **5.** larger
6. smaller

TEACHING STRATEGIES

Summary: Susan B. Anthony, Elizabeth Cady Stanton, Jane Addams, Janie Porter Barrett, Lillian Wald, and Alice Hamilton improved life in America.

Objective: Students will understand how six women worked for women's rights and to improve the conditions of America's schools, factories, and neighborhoods.

Pre-Reading Activities: **1.** Discuss how schools, kindergartens, and day care facilities help children and their parents. **2.** Ask students to list ways that someone might help a new immigrant. **3.** Remind students how labor unions and a photographer helped improve factory conditions. Ask students how they think a doctor might be able to help make a factory safer.

Vocabulary Activities: **1.** Help students choose the correct definition and pronunciation for the word *lead* as used in the chapter. **2.** Ask students to use each new word in a sentence.

Review Words
(Bk 2, Chaps. 1–7; CE, Chaps. 22–28) immigrants, salaries
(Bk 1 and CE, Chaps. 1–21) citizens, amendments

Post-Reading Discussion Points: **1.** Ask students why the six women from the chapter wanted to help other people. Discuss how job satisfaction can be important in the choice of a career. **2.** Discuss with students how the efforts of one person, such as Jane Addams, can make a difference in the lives of many people. **3.** Discuss with students how the efforts of one person, such as Lillian Wald, can make a difference in the lives of people decades to hundreds of years later. To illustrate this point, ask how many students have seen the school nurse.

Primary Source Quote: In 1931 Jane Addams was awarded the Nobel Peace Prize for her work to improve the lives of children, immigrants, and factory workers.

ELL Activity: Have student groups choose one woman who worked for change in America. Have groups work cooperatively to learn all they can about their choice from the textbook and other sources. Then have group members take turns answering *yes* or *no* as other groups ask questions to discover the woman's name. If a student cannot answer a question, have him or her work with group members to find the answer.

Primary Source Activities: **1.** Review the meaning of the vocabulary words with the students. **2.** Read to the students primary source materials written by the other women in the chapter or by child laborers.

Follow-Up Activities: **1.** Have students write to the Jane Addams Center (3212 N. Broadway, Chicago, IL 60657) or the Henry Street Settlement House (265 Henry St., New York, NY 10002) to learn about what the Hull House and the Henry Street Settlement House are doing today.

Chapter Online Resources:
Find more information about topics in this chapter at *www.HarcourtAchieve.com/AchievementZone.* Click on *America's Story.*

ANSWER KEY

Learning from Pictures (Bk 2, p. 50; CE, p. 194)
She is teaching them to read.

Using Primary Sources (Bk 2, p. 53; CE, p. 197)
1. Italians, Germans, Polish and Russian Jews
2. They were built for one family, but housed several. Many had no water supply or no fire escapes.
3. because they worked long hours in a candy factory and did not want to look at the candy
4. seven in the morning until nine at night for six weeks **5. Constructed Response:** Answers will vary. Students should point out that Hull House tried to make life better for children by letting others know of the poor conditions in which children were living and working.

Using What You've Learned

Who Am I? (Bk 2, p. 54; CE, p. 198)
1. Elizabeth Cady Stanton **2.** Susan B. Anthony **3.** Jane Addams **4.** Janie Porter Barrett **5.** Lillian Wald **6.** Alice Hamilton

Fact or Opinion (Bk 2, p. 54; CE, p. 198)
1. O **2.** F **3.** F **4.** O **5.** F **6.** F **(CE) 7.** O

TEACHING STRATEGIES

Summary: Various Americans tried to solve some of America's problems in the early 1900s.

Objective: Students will learn about the contributions made by Americans who worked for reform in the United States in the early 1900s.

Pre-Reading Activities: 1. Have students look at the pictures in this chapter. Ask them to identify some of the problems that faced Americans in the early 1900s.   **2.** Ask students to recall how Jacob Riis and Jane Addams helped poor immigrants in American cities. Then tell students that in this chapter they will learn about the contributions of other Americans who helped solve America's problems in the early 1900s.

Vocabulary Activities: 1. Discuss the meaning of each new word.   **2.** Have students write a paragraph that includes several vocabulary words.

Review Words
(Bk 2, Chaps. 1–8; CE, Chaps. 22–29)
   salaries, strike, working conditions, labor unions, immigrants, big business, equal rights, child labor, employers
(Bk 1 and CE, Chaps. 1–21) reform, Supreme Court, Congress, religions, nation, disabilities

Post-Reading Discussion Points: 1. Ask students to describe the problems facing Americans in the early 1900s and how these problems were solved.
2. Ask students to explain how muckrakers worked to correct problems in American life.

Primary Source Quote: In *The History of the Standard Oil Company* Ida Tarbell exposed the illegal ways in which John D. Rockefeller monopolized the early oil industry.

ELL Activity: Have groups write questions and answers describing people who worked for reform from Chapter 30. Then have groups trade answers and try to guess which questions go with the answers.

Follow-Up Activities: 1. Have students use the Sequencing graphic organizer on page 110 of this guide to show how progressives worked for reform.

Chapter Online Resources:
Find more information about topics in this chapter at *www.HarcourtAchieve.com/AchievementZone.* Click on *America's Story.*

ANSWER KEY

Learning from Pictures (Bk 2, p. 57; CE, p. 201)
Answers will vary, but should include that it was dangerous, crowded, dirty, and they worked in smelly conditions.

Using What You've Learned

Write the Answer (Bk 2, p. 59; CE, p. 203)
1. Kelley got the Supreme Court to agree to a law that said employers could not make women work more than 10 hours a day.   **2.** President Roosevelt helped end the coal miners' strike. He said mine owners must work with the union to give workers better working conditions.
3. A muckraker was a person who tried to solve American problems by writing about them in a book, newspaper, or magazine.   **4.** The Supreme Court ruled that it was against the law for Standard Oil to control America's oil. Thirty-three smaller companies were formed.   **5.** He wrote about problems in America's meat industry.   **(CE) 6.** The Pure Food and Drug Act was a law that said all food and medicine must be safe for people to use.   **(CE) 7.** President Roosevelt worked with Congress to pass laws to protect forests.
(CE) 8. Answers should include any one of the following: There were laws that made it hard for African Americans to vote. African American children were not allowed to go to school with white children. It was hard for African Americans to get good jobs.
(CE) 9. Florence Kelley worked with Du Bois and Addams at the NAACP.

Categories (Bk 2, p. 59; CE, p. 203)
1. Theodore Roosevelt   **2.** Florence Kelley
3. W.E.B. Du Bois   **4.** Muckrakers

Reading a Circle Graph (Bk 2, p. 60; CE, p. 204)
1. six   **2.** farm   **3.** largest   **4.** smallest   **5.** factory
6. half

Journal Writing (Bk 2, p. 60; CE, p. 204)
Paragraphs will vary. Students should choose a person who worked for reform in the early 1900s and tell why the work was important.

Name _____

◄ UNIT REVIEW ►

THE UNITED STATES BECOMES A MODERN NATION

Choose the Answer Use the time line from the unit opener to answer the questions below. Draw a circle around the correct answer.

1. When did Jane Addams start Hull House?
   1889   1906   1911

2. Who was arrested for trying to vote in 1872?
   Susan B. Anthony   Samuel Gompers   W.E.B. Du Bois

3. In what year was oil found in Pennsylvania?
   1859   1886   1899

4. Which event happened first?
   Andrew Carnegie owned most of America's steel companies.
   Samuel Gompers helped start the AFL.
   John D. Rockefeller built his first oil refinery.

Match Up Finish each sentence in Group A with words from Group B. Write the letter of the correct answer on the blank line.

Group A

1. _____ was a famous union leader.

2. _____ proved that workers got sick from lead poisoning.

3. _____ started a program of visiting nurses in New York City.

4. _____ inspected factories to make sure they were safe.

5. _____ was an immigrant from Denmark who helped other immigrants by writing news stories.

Group B

a. Florence Kelley

b. Jacob Riis

c. Samuel Gompers

d. Alice Hamilton

e. Lillian Wald

Name _____

◀ UNIT REVIEW ▶

THE UNITED STATES BECOMES A MODERN NATION

Riddle Review   Use a word in dark print to complete each sentence below. Write the word on the blanks next to each sentence.

railroads	Tarbell	Hine	Pure
millionaire	Jones	slaves	Barrett

1. Immigrants from China and Ireland helped build the _____ .

   __ ☐ __ __ __ __ __ __

2. Lewis _____ helped children in factories with his photographs.

   __ ☐ __ __

3. Janie Porter _____ started a school for African American girls who had been in jail.

   __ __ ☐ __ __ __ __

4. The _____ Food and Drug Act helped make food and medicine safe for Americans.

   ☐ __ __ __

5. Owning steel mills helped Andrew Carnegie become a _____ .

   __ __ __ ☐ __ __ __ __ __ __

6. African Americans were forced to come to America as _____ .

   __ __ ☐ __ __ __

7. The Irish immigrant who helped factory workers and miners was called "Mother" _____ .

   __ __ ☐ __ __

8. Ida _____ wanted the government to do more to control big business.

   __ __ __ ☐ __ __

The letters in the box spell a word. The word answers the riddle.

RIDDLE: What can a person use to go faster than a car or train without using his or her legs?

ANSWER: __ __ __ __ __ __ __

Name _____

◁ UNIT TEST ▷

THE UNITED STATES BECOMES A MODERN NATION

True or False   Write **T** next to each sentence that is true. Write **F** next to each sentence that is false.

_____ 1. John D. Rockefeller owned many oil companies in America.

_____ 2. Alice Hamilton worked to make factories safer for workers.

_____ 3. Our laws today allow union workers to go on strike.

_____ 4. Most immigrants from Italy, Russia, and Poland were rich.

_____ 5. President Theodore Roosevelt worked to protect America's natural resources.

_____ 6. Jacob Riis wrote newspaper stories about immigrant life.

Match Up   Finish each sentence in Group A with words from Group B. Write the letter of the correct answer on the blank line.

Group A

1. The Locust Street Social Settlement House was in _____ .

2. Oil is cleaned in oil _____ .

3. Many immigrants worked long hours in _____ .

4. Before the 1880s, many immigrants came from _____ .

5. W.E.B. Du Bois started the _____ to help end discrimination against African Americans.

Group B

a. refineries

b. Virginia

c. NAACP

d. Great Britain and Germany

e. factories

Name _____

◀ UNIT TEST ▶

THE UNITED STATES BECOMES A MODERN NATION

Sequencing Events   Write the numbers **1**, **2**, **3**, **4**, and **5** next to these sentences to show the correct order.

_____   John D. Rockefeller built his first oil refinery.

_____   The Pure Food and Drug Act was passed.

_____   W.E.B. Du Bois helped start the NAACP in 1909.

_____   In 1895 Lillian Wald started the Henry Street Settlement House.

_____   People in Ireland were starving in the 1840s.

Finish the Sentence   Draw a circle around the word or words that finish each sentence.

1. Andrew Carnegie owned _____ .
   car factories   steel mills   oil refineries

2. _____ took photographs of children who worked in factories.
   Jane Addams   Alice Hamilton   Lewis Hine

3. The muckraker who wrote about problems in the meat industry was _____ .
   Florence Kelley   Theodore Roosevelt   Upton Sinclair

4. _____ came to the United States for a different reason than any other immigrant group.
   African Americans   Irish Americans   German Americans

5. Mary Jones helped miners start labor _____ .
   newspapers   unions   factories

6. In 1886 _____ helped start the American Federation of Labor.
   Janie Porter Barrett   Ida Tarbell   Samuel Gompers

TEACHING STRATEGIES

Summary: The United States helped the Allies win World War I in 1918 and World War II in 1945. The 1920s was a time of many changes in the United States. The Great Depression ended when World War II began.

Major Concepts:
- **Civics:** The Nineteenth Amendment gave women the right to vote in 1920.
- **Economics:** People began to buy new machines on credit. Americans began buying shares of stock. The stock market crashed, helping cause the Great Depression.
- **Geography:** A long drought caused the Great Plains to become known as the Dust Bowl.
- **Government:** Franklin D. Roosevelt presented the New Deal, a series of programs to help end the Great Depression. Americans feared communism would win control in the United States.
- **History:** The industrial and military strengths of the United States helped the Allies win the world wars. The dropping of two atomic bombs forced Japan to surrender.

Pre-Reading Activities: 1. Remind students that after the Civil War the right to vote was given to African American men. Discuss the fact that women were still not allowed to vote. **2.** Show students photographs or other memorabilia from the 1910s through 1940s. Ask students to describe things that are different from modern photos, such as clothing and hairstyles. **3.** Have students look at the time line in the unit opener. Ask them to calculate about how many years of American history this unit covers. Then ask them to predict the main ideas of the unit based on the information in the unit time line, the title of the unit, and the picture in the unit opener.

Post-Reading Discussion Points: 1. Ask students to explain how World War I may have helped cause World War II. **2.** Discuss with students the role of World War I in Americans' desire for isolation. **3.** Discuss with students the promises made between the United States and its allies. Help students understand how these promises affected America's involvement in World War I and World War II.

Follow-Up Activities: 1. Have students learn more about the government programs begun under the New Deal. **2.** Have students report on the many changes during the 1920s in the United States. **3.** Have students use the Sequencing graphic organizer on page 110 of this guide to show the sequence of major events in the United States from 1910 to 1945. **4.** Have students discuss why technology develops rapidly during times of war. Suggest that they think about communication, aviation, and weapons.

Review Activities: Refer to pages 80–81 of this guide for review activities covering this unit.

Assessment: Refer to pages 82–83 of this guide for the Unit Test.

ANSWER KEY

Unit Review (Bk 2, p. 97; CE, p. 241)
1. 1918 **2.** Central Powers **3.** Constitution **4.** vote **5.** stock market **6.** Depression **7.** New Deal **8.** 1939 **9.** Japan

Unit Review (Teacher's Guide, pp. 80–81)

Choose the Answer 1. 1914 **2.** An amendment was added that allowed women to vote. **3.** 1929 **4.** 1941

Match Up 1. e **2.** a **3.** c **4.** b **5.** d

Riddle Review 1. prince **2.** credit **3.** popular **4.** Hitler **5.** German **6.** shares **7.** Pearl
Answer: N E U T R A L

Unit Test (Teacher's Guide, pp. 82–83)

True or False 1. F **2.** T **3.** T **4.** F **5.** T **6.** F

Match Up 1. b **2.** e **3.** a **4.** c **5.** d

Sequencing Events The sentences should be numbered 4, 3, 1, 5, 2.

Finish the Sentence 1. Europe **2.** Austria-Hungary **3.** the Soviet Union **4.** farmers grew more crops than they could sell **5.** Jews **6.** France

TEACHING STRATEGIES

Summary: The United States entered World War I in 1917 after Germany sank American ships. The United States and the Allies won the war in 1918.

Objective: Students will learn the causes and results of World War I and American involvement in the war.

Pre-Reading Activities: **1.** Have students use the map in this chapter to answer questions such as the following: Was Russia one of the Allies or one of the Central Powers? What were two neutral countries? **2.** Have students compare the map in this chapter with a current map of Europe. Discuss how wars can lead to changes in national boundaries. Have students recall earlier wars that affected the boundaries of the United States.

Vocabulary Activities: Discuss the meanings of the vocabulary words. Ask students to use the meanings to create questions about this chapter.

Review Words
(Bk 2, Chaps. 1–9; CE, Chaps. 22–30) imperialism, weapons
(Bk 1 and CE, Chaps. 1–21) Congress, captured, peace treaty, citizens, surrendered

Post-Reading Discussion Points: **1.** Discuss the causes of World War I. Point out that the killing of the prince was only one cause of the war. **2.** Discuss the treatment received by German Americans during World War I. Was it fair? **3.** Ask students to compare Germany's attack on American ships in World War I to Great Britain's attack on American ships in the War of 1812.

Primary Source Quote: President Woodrow Wilson delivered this speech in a joint session of Congress on January 8, 1918.

ELL Activity: Have students label on a map the Allies in World War I. Then have students tell why the United States became involved in the war.

Follow-Up Activities: **1.** Have students use the Event Description graphic organizer on page 110 of this guide to describe important information about World War I. In the center box, have students write *World War I.* Students should complete the rest of the organizer with information from the chapter.

Chapter Online Resources:
Find more information about topics in this chapter at *www.HarcourtAchieve.com/AchievementZone.* Click on *America's Story.*

ANSWER KEY

Learning from Pictures (Bk 2, p. 64; CE, p. 208)
Answers will vary, but should include that World War I soldiers did not have the protective clothing and advanced weapons of soldiers today.

Using Maps (Bk 2, p. 65; CE, p. 209)
Students should list two of the following: Turkey, Austria-Hungary, Bulgaria, or Germany.

Using What You've Learned

Finish the Story (Bk 2, p. 68; CE, p. 212)
1. 1914 **2.** Woodrow Wilson **3.** neutral **4.** Allies
5. American **6.** 1917 **7.** Paris **8.** surrendered

Using Graphic Organizers: Main Idea and Supporting Details (Bk 2, pp. 68–69; CE, pp. 212–213)
1. Some nations in Europe promised to fight for one another in a war. **2.** World War I began after a person from Serbia killed the prince of Austria-Hungary.
3. The United States wanted to help the Allies win the war. **4.** Americans wanted to help during the war.
(CE) 5. Germany surrendered to the Allies.

Reading a Historical Map (Bk 2, p. 69; CE, p. 213)
1. Students should name four of the following: Russia, Italy, Great Britain, Romania, Serbia, France.
2. Students should name three of the following: Germany, Austria-Hungary, Turkey, Bulgaria.
3. Students should name four of the following: Norway, Sweden, Spain, Switzerland, Denmark.
4. Russia **(CE) 5.** Russia

Journal Writing (Bk 2, p. 69; CE, p. 213)
Paragraphs will vary. Students might mention that not all German Americans liked Germany, that German Americans were still American citizens, that it was not a good reason for an American to lose a job, or that people should not be treated a certain way just because they or their ancestors came from a certain country.

TEACHING STRATEGIES

Summary: Women won the right to vote; machines made life easier; and radio, movies, and sports entertained people. Americans traveled in cars and airplanes. Also, many farmers lost their farms. The Ku Klux Klan and communism increased the fears of Americans.

Objective: Students will learn how the United States changed during the 1920s.

Pre-Reading Activities: **1.** Have students study the pictures and captions in this chapter. Ask them what these pictures tell them about changes in the United States during the 1920s. **2.** Read a poem by Langston Hughes to the class.

Vocabulary Activities: Have students work in pairs to find meanings for the vocabulary words.

Review Words
(Bk 2, Chaps. 1–10; CE, Chaps. 22–31) weapons, immigrants
(Bk 1 and CE, Chaps. 1–21) amendments, Constitution, in debt, nation, crops, goods

Post-Reading Discussion Points: **1.** Discuss why many Americans wanted isolation after World War I. **2.** Discuss the ways new machines made home life easier for Americans. **3.** Ask students to discuss the problems that the people of the United States faced during the 1920s.

Primary Source Quote: This quote comes from an essay entitled, "The Negro Artist and the Racial Mountain" in which Langston Hughes wrote of African American writers and poets.

ELL Activity: Have students listen to jazz music. Ask students to list reasons why they think jazz became popular during the 1920s.

Geography Theme Activities: **1.** Have students research how long it takes airmail to fly from San Francisco to New York City today. Have them calculate the difference in airmail travel time today with that of 1921. **2.** Provide students with outline maps of the United States on page 123 of this guide. Have students make maps of major air routes in the United States today.

Follow-Up Activities: **1.** Ask students to report on the life of Langston Hughes or Charles Lindbergh.

2. Help students use the Concept Web graphic organizer on page 109 of this guide to show information about the Harlem Renaissance. Have students write *Harlem Renaissance* in the center of the web. Then have them write supporting information on the spokes of the web.

Chapter Online Resources:
Find more information about topics in this chapter at *www.HarcourtAchieve.com/AchievementZone.* Click on *America's Story.*

ANSWER KEY

Learning from Pictures (Bk 2, p. 71; CE, p. 215)
Answers will vary, but should include that in the 1920s machines were larger, the clothes had to be rung out separately when the wash was finished, and a load of laundry took a long time; today machines are smaller, the clothes are washed, rinsed, and have the water spun out of them in the same cycle, and a load of laundry takes less time.

Using Geography Themes (Bk 2, p. 75; CE, p. 219)
1. on trains **2.** Philadelphia **3.** on trains **4.** 2,666 miles **5.** Students should name any four of the following: Reno, Salt Lake City, Chicago, Cleveland, New York City. **6.** Los Angeles

Using What You've Learned

Find the Answers (Bk 2, p. 76; CE, p. 220)
Students should choose the following sentences:
1. Americans wanted the United States to be isolated from Europe after World War I. **2.** The Nineteenth Amendment gave women the right to vote. **3.** People bought new machines on credit. **6.** Communism and the Ku Klux Klan brought fear to Americans.

Fact or Opinion (Bk 2, p. 76; CE, p. 220)
1. O **2.** F **3.** O **4.** F **5.** O **6.** F **7.** F **8.** O **9.** F **10.** F

Reading a Time Line (Bk 2, p. 77; CE, p. 221)
1. the Soviet Union **2.** 1921 and 1924 **3.** 1927 **4.** before

Journal Writing (Bk 2, p. 77; CE, p. 221)
Answers will vary. Students should choose two ways people had fun in the 1920s and write four to five sentences about them.

TEACHING STRATEGIES

Summary: America entered its longest and hardest depression in 1929. Franklin D. Roosevelt's New Deal and jobs created by World War II helped end the Great Depression.

Objective: Students will understand the causes of the Great Depression and the programs started by the government to help end the depression.

Pre-Reading Activities: 1. Have students study the pictures and captions in this chapter. Ask them to compare the price of the man's car to today's car prices. 2. Ask students what it would be like if most Americans did not have jobs, money, homes, or food. Ask students to make suggestions about how to end such a problem.

Vocabulary Activities: 1. Have students use each new vocabulary word correctly in a sentence. 2. Discuss other meanings for the words *depression, stock,* and *crashed.*

Review Words
(Bk 2, Chaps. 1–11; CE, Chaps. 22–32) salaries,
    popular, weapons
(Bk 1 and CE, Chaps. 1–21) nation, crops, Congress

Post-Reading Discussion Points: 1. Discuss why the government paid farmers to grow less food. 2. Ask students to discuss the stock market crash. Clarify any confusion about stocks. 3. Have students describe the New Deal. 4. Ask students why they think Franklin D. Roosevelt was elected President four times.

Primary Source Quote: President Franklin D. Roosevelt delivered this radio address from the White House on May 7, 1933.

ELL Activity: Help students list causes and effects related to the Great Depression on paper strips and make a paper chain by joining each cause to its effect. Guide students to see that many linked causes led to the Great Depression, and that a chain of effects made the Depression worse.

Follow-Up Activities: 1. Play an audio recording of Franklin D. Roosevelt's speech in which he said, "The only thing we have to fear is fear itself." Have the class discuss why Roosevelt made this speech. 2. Invite a local resource person to speak to the class and answer questions about what it was like to live in America during the Great Depression. Have students write summaries about the discussion. 3. Have students research and report on some of the historic preservation programs of the New Deal.

Chapter Online Resources:
Find more information about topics in this chapter at *www.HarcourtAchieve.com/AchievementZone.* Click on *America's Story.*

ANSWER KEY

Learning from Pictures (Bk 2, p. 80; CE, p. 224)
Answers will vary, but should include that they are hungry and probably don't have enough money to buy their own food.

Using What You've Learned

True or False (Bk 2, p. 82; CE, p. 226)
1. T **2.** F **3.** T **4.** F **5.** T

Using Graphic Organizers: Cause and Effect
(Bk 2, p. 82; CE, p. 226)
1. b **2.** a **3.** c

Using a Map Key (Bk 2, p. 83; CE, p. 227)
Students should choose the following sentences:
1. Tennessee, Mississippi, and Alabama receive electricity from the TVA. **3.** Kentucky, Virginia, and Georgia receive electricity from the TVA. **5.** The TVA has dams on the Cumberland and Tennessee rivers.

Journal Writing (Bk 2, p. 83; CE, p. 227)
Answers will vary. Students may mention that the photograph shows many people standing in line waiting for food. The students may also describe the people's clothing or the dishes on the table. Students should write that the photograph shows that many people became poor during the Great Depression, and that many people needed food.

TEACHING STRATEGIES

Summary: Germany started World War II in 1939. The United States entered the war when Japan attacked Pearl Harbor in 1941.

Objective: Students will understand the causes of World War II and America's entry into the war.

Pre-Reading Activities: 1. Ask students to compare and contrast the map from the chapter on World War I with the map in this chapter. **2.** Point out that World War II began only 21 years after the end of World War I. Many soldiers fought in both wars. Discuss how people might have felt about another war.

Vocabulary Activities: Have students locate the sentences in the chapter in which bold-faced words appear. Help them use the context of the sentences to learn the meaning of each new word.

Review Words
(Bk 2, Chaps. 1–12; CE, Chaps. 22–33)
  Great Depression, neutral, Allies, weapons, declared war
(Bk 1 and CE, Chaps. 1–21) captured, escape, nation, destroyed, goal, surrendered, peace treaty, colony

Post-Reading Discussion Points: 1. Ask students to identify the causes of World War II. Why did America get involved? **2.** Tell students that in addition to the six million Jews killed during the Holocaust, millions of other people, including Germans who opposed Hitler, were also killed. **3.** Ask students to contrast a dictatorship to a government where leaders are elected by the people.

Primary Source Quote: Winston Churchill spoke these words to the House of Commons in Great Britain on June 4, 1940 in an attempt to appeal to the United States for aid.

ELL Activity: Have students identify Axis and Allied countries on a wall battle map and use pins, string, labels, or other methods to show the progress of the war on the map as they read Chapters 34 and 35.

Primary Source Activities: 1. Have students find other examples of political cartoons from World War II. Display the cartoons on a bulletin board in the classroom. **2.** Have students find political cartoons in newspapers and magazines about political issues today. Ask students to share the cartoons and discuss their meanings.

Follow-Up Activities: 1. Read passages from *The Diary of Anne Frank* to the students. **2.** Have students use the Geography Theme: Place blackline master on page 116 of this guide to describe Pearl Harbor, Hawaii. Students should use outside resources to complete this activity.

Chapter Online Resources:
Find more information about topics in this chapter at *www.HarcourtAchieve.com/AchievementZone.* Click on *America's Story.*

ANSWER KEY

Using Maps (Bk 2, p.85 ; CE, p. 229)
Spain and Switzerland

Learning from Pictures (Bk 2, p. 87; CE, p. 231)
He has many medals on his uniform.

Using Primary Sources (Bk 2, p. 88; CE, p. 232)
1. Poland **2.** Answers may vary, but should indicate that Germany plans to crush, overrun, conquer, or take over Poland. **3.** 1939 **4.** a dangerous place **5. Constructed Response:** Answers may vary, but should indicate that the artist showed that Germany was very powerful by making the swastika very big.

Using What You've Learned

Choose the Answer (Bk 2, p. 89; CE, p. 233)
1. appeasement **2.** 1939 **3.** 6 million **4.** Great Britain **5.** Japan **(CE) 6.** 1941

Understanding Different Points of View
(Bk 2, p. 89; CE, p. 233)
1. Axis **2.** Axis **3.** Allies **4.** Allies **5.** Axis **6.** Allies

Reading a Chart (Bk 2, p. 90; CE, p. 234)
1. Allies **2.** Great Britain **3.** Canada **4.** Switzerland and Sweden **5.** Allies **6.** neutral countries **7.** Japan

TEACHING STRATEGIES

Summary: The United States and the Allies defeated the Axis countries in 1945. The United States used two atomic bombs to force Japan to surrender, ending the war.

Objective: Students will understand how the United States helped defeat the Axis powers and how World War II affected Americans.

Pre-Reading Activities: 1. Help students use a wall map to locate sites of major battles during World War II: Paris, Berlin, Hiroshima, Nagasaki, the Philippines, and Guam. **2.** Ask students to tell what they know about the invention and the use of the atomic bomb.

Vocabulary Activities: Have students make crossword puzzles using as many of the chapter's vocabulary words as possible. Then have students exchange and solve the puzzles.

Review Words
(Bk 2, Chaps. 1–13; CE, Chaps. 22–34)
    Axis countries, conquer, bombs, Allies, Great Depression, weapons
(Bk 1 and CE, Chaps. 1–21) nation, crops, captured, destroyed, general, surrendered

Post-Reading Discussion Points: 1. Have students tell why American farmers were so important in World War II. **2.** Military leaders estimated that an invasion of Japan would have lead to half a million American casualties. Discuss President Truman's decision to use the atomic bomb to force Japan to surrender. **3.** Ask students to compare the treatment of German Americans during World War I to that of Japanese Americans during World War II. **4.** Ask students if they would be willing to ration goods such as meat, sugar, flour, and gasoline to aid a war effort.

Primary Source Quote: Allen W. Stephens was a pilot with the 397th Bomb Group during World War II.

ELL Activity: Have students create a wall time line from 1930 to 1945 increasing in five-year increments. Divide students into groups. Have each group add an event to the time line from Chapter 34 and 35.

Follow-Up Activities: 1. Have students debate whether President Truman was correct in his decision to use the atomic bomb. **2.** Have a local resource person speak to the class about life in the United States during World War II. **3.** Help students use the Concept Web graphic organizer on page 109 of this

guide to summarize American involvement in World War II. In the center have students write *American Involvement in World War II*. On the spokes, have students write ways Americans became involved in World War II. Have students use information from this chapter and the previous chapter, "World War II Begins."

Chapter Online Resources:
Find more information about topics in this chapter at *www.HarcourtAchieve.com/AchievementZone*. Click on *America's Story*.

ANSWER KEY

Learning from Pictures (Bk 2, p. 91; CE, p. 235)
Answers will vary, but should include that the United States probably won an important battle at Iwo Jima.

Using Maps (Bk 2, p. 94; CE, p. 238)
Hiroshima and Nagasaki

Using What You've Learned

Choose a Word (Bk 2, p. 95; CE, p. 239)
1. rationed **2.** tanks **3.** metal **4.** Eisenhower **5.** surrendered **6.** MacArthur **7.** Truman **8.** World War II

Drawing Conclusions (Bk 2, pp. 95–96; CE, pp. 239–240)
1. c **2.** b **3.** d **4.** a **(CE) 5.** f **(CE) 6.** e

Reading a Historical Map (Bk 2, p. 96; CE, p. 240)
1. China **2.** Students should name two of the following places: Philippines, Guam, Pearl Harbor, Iwo Jima. **3.** Hiroshima and Nagasaki **4.** Pearl Harbor, Hawaii **(CE) 5.** 11 **(CE) 6.** Australia

Journal Writing (Bk 2, p. 96; CE, p. 240)
Answers will vary. Paragraphs should list three of the following: women worked in factories to make ships, airplanes, guns, tanks, and clothing for soldiers; farmers worked hard to grow extra food; people rationed foods, such as meat, sugar, and flour; people collected old metal.

Name _____

◄ UNIT REVIEW ►

PROBLEMS AT HOME AND ACROSS THE SEA

Choose the Answer   Use the time line from the unit opener to answer the questions below. Draw a circle around the correct answer.

1. In what year did World War I begin?
   1914   1918   1939

2. What happened in 1920?
   The United States began to fight in World War I.
   An amendment was added that allowed women to vote.
   Adolf Hitler became the leader of Germany.

3. The stock market crashed and the Great Depression began in what year?
   1917   1929   1941

4. When did the United States begin to fight in World War II?
   1927   1939   1941

Match Up   Finish each sentence in Group A with words from Group B. Write the letter of the correct answer on the blank line.

Group A

1. In World War I, the United States and the Allies fought against the _____ .

2. _____ was the leader of Great Britain during World War II.

3. _____ was the first person to fly alone across the Atlantic Ocean.

4. Franklin D. Roosevelt started the _____ to try to end the Great Depression.

5. President _____ decided to use the atomic bomb in World War II.

Group B

a. Winston Churchill

b. New Deal

c. Charles Lindbergh

d. Harry S Truman

e. Central Powers

Name _____

◄ UNIT REVIEW ►

PROBLEMS AT HOME AND ACROSS THE SEA

Riddle Review   Use a word in dark print to complete each sentence below. Write the word on the blanks next to each sentence.

credit	**shares**	**Hitler**	**prince**
popular	**German**	**Pearl**	

1. In 1914 the _____ of Austria-Hungary was killed.

   _ _ _ ☐ _ _

2. People without enough money bought new machines on _____ .

   _ _ ☐ _ _ _

3. Herbert Hoover was not a _____ President.

   _ _ _ ☐ _ _ _

4. Adolf _____ was the leader of Germany during World War II.

   _ _ ☐ _ _ _

5. _____ Americans were treated unfairly during World War I.

   _ _ ☐ _ _ _

6. When you buy stock, you own _____ in a company.

   _ _ ☐ _ _ _

7. The United States entered World War II after the Japanese attacked _____ Harbor.

   _ _ _ _ _ ☐

The letters in the boxes spell a word. The word answers the riddle.

RIDDLE: If you don't take sides, what are you?

ANSWER: _ _ _ _ _ _ _

Name _____

◢ UNIT TEST ◣

PROBLEMS AT HOME AND ACROSS THE SEA

True or False   Write **T** next to each sentence that is true. Write **F** next to each sentence that is false.

_____ 1. The United States helped the Central Powers during World War I.

_____ 2. During the Great Depression, Roosevelt paid the farmers to grow less food.

_____ 3. Japanese Americans fought for the United States during World War II.

_____ 4. The United States dropped two atomic bombs on German cities to end World War II.

_____ 5. During the Harlem Renaissance, African Americans created new art and music.

_____ 6. Germany captured Great Britain during World War II.

Match Up   Finish each sentence in Group A with words from Group B. Write the letter of the correct answer on the blank line.

Group A

1. The _____ won World War I.

2. Germany, Japan, and _____ were the Axis countries during World War II.

3. General _____ led the American troops in the Philippines.

4. The 1920 amendment that allowed women to vote was the _____ Amendment.

5. _____ was elected President four times.

Group B

a. Douglas MacArthur

b. Allies

c. Nineteenth

d. Franklin D. Roosevelt

e. Italy

82

Name _____

◀ UNIT TEST ▶

PROBLEMS AT HOME AND ACROSS THE SEA

Sequencing Events   Write the numbers **1**, **2**, **3**, **4**, and **5** next to these sentences to show the correct order.

_____   Germany dropped many bombs on Great Britain in 1940.

_____   In 1929 the stock market crashed.

_____   The Central Powers surrendered to the Allies.

_____   The United States began to fight in World War II.

_____   In 1927 Charles Lindbergh became the first person to fly alone across the Atlantic Ocean.

Finish the Sentence   Draw a circle around the word or words that finish each sentence.

1. Most of World War I was fought in _____ .
   Europe   the Philippines   the United States

2. _____ was one of the Central Powers during World War I.
   Serbia   Russia   Austria-Hungary

3. In 1922 Russia and some other countries formed a Communist nation called _____ .
   Iwo Jima   the Soviet Union   Czechoslovakia

4. One cause of the Great Depression was _____ .
   farmers grew more crops than they could sell
   workers had too much money
   factories did not have enough workers

5. Hitler had six million _____ killed in concentration camps.
   Jews   Japanese Americans   British soldiers

6. General Eisenhower led the Allied soldiers to free _____ from Germany during World War II.
   Guam   France   Spain

TEACHING STRATEGIES

Summary: After World War II, America worked to prevent the spread of communism during the Cold War. Advances were made in the fields of medicine and space exploration. Many people fought for civil rights for all Americans. Others worked to improve working conditions for migrant farm workers.

Major Concepts:
- **Geography:** After World War II, Americans began moving from cities to suburbs.
- **Government:** During the Cold War, the United States government tried to prevent the spread of communism and to encourage democracy.
- **History:** The Vietnam War lasted longer than any other war Americans had fought in. The race with the Soviet Union to control space led to the landing of Americans on the moon.
- **Sociology:** Americans fought for civil rights, helped migrant farm workers, and protested a war by boycotting and marching. New medicines helped Americans become healthier.

Pre-Reading Activities: 1. Explain that even though the United States and the Soviet Union were allies in World War II, the two nations became enemies after the war because of their differing governments and goals. 2. Discuss the First Amendment. Ask students how the rights to freedom of speech and peaceful assembly might be used by Americans to change things they believe are unfair.

Post-Reading Discussion Points: 1. Discuss some of the major events that occurred during the Cold War. 2. Ask students to imagine a cause for which they would be willing to strike, march, or boycott. 3. Discuss the reasons for and the results of the space race. Ask students if they think the risks and the expense of the space program are worth the gains.

Follow-Up Activities: 1. Invite students to learn more about the United Farm Workers today. 2. Have students use the Feature Chart graphic organizer on page 113 of this guide to compare the civil rights movement, the migrant farm workers movement, and the movement against the war in Vietnam. What methods did each movement use? What changes did the movement bring about? 3. Have the class watch a live or taped launching of the space shuttle.

Review Activities: Refer to pages 91–92 of this guide for review activities covering this unit.

Assessment: Refer to pages 93–94 of this guide for the Unit Test.

ANSWER KEY

Unit Review (Bk 2, p. 135; CE, p. 279)
1. Cold War 2. Berlin Wall 3. Cuba 4. South Vietnam 5. Communist 6. Supreme Court 7. strike 8. moon 9. shuttle

Unit Review (Teacher's Guide, pp. 91–92)

Choose the Answer 1. 1965 2. The Korean War ended. 3. César Chávez 4. 1975

Match Up 1. c 2. e 3. a 4. b 5. d

Riddle Review 1. bus 2. school 3. spray 4. Cold 5. moon 6. protests 7. McCarthy
Answer: B O Y C O T T

Unit Test (Teacher's Guide, pp. 93–94)

True or False 1. F 2. T 3. T 4. T 5. T 6. T

Match Up 1. b 2. c 3. a 4. e 5. d

Sequencing Events The sentences should be numbered 5, 2, 4, 3, 1.

Finish the Sentence 1. segregation 2. NATO 3. too many American soldiers were being killed 4. space race 5. Martin Luther King, Jr. 6. to help migrant farm workers

TEACHING STRATEGIES

Summary: The United States and the Soviet Union fought the Cold War over the spread of communism.

Objective: Students will understand the goals of the United States after World War II and the causes of the Cold War. They will learn the differences between a Communist government and a democracy, and they will learn about the creation of the United Nations and NATO.

Pre-Reading Activities: **1.** Have students locate on a world map the United States, the former Soviet Union, Cuba, Germany, China, and North and South Korea. **2.** Point out that conflicts over kinds of government caused actual fighting in Korea and political battles in Germany and Cuba.

Vocabulary Activities: **1.** Write NATO on the chalkboard. Tell students that the letters stand for North Atlantic Treaty Organization. Explain that this kind of abbreviation is called an acronym. Remind students of the acronym AFL (American Federation of Labor). **2.** Have students write a story using the new words.

Review Words
(Bk 2, Chaps. 1–14; CE, Chaps. 22–35) dictator,
   weapons, communism, invaded
(Bk 1 and CE, Chaps. 1–21) nation, rebuild, capital,
   destroyed, escape, freedom of religion, goal

Post-Reading Discussion Points: **1.** Discuss the ideas of democracy and communism. How did these ideas lead to the Cold War? **2.** Have students compare the Korean War with the conflicts in Germany and Cuba. **3.** Have students discuss the participation of the United Nations in the Cold War.

Primary Source Quote: President John F. Kennedy spoke these words during a radio and television announcement from the White House on October 22, 1962 about the Soviet arms buildup in Cuba.

ELL Activity: Discuss the term *Cold War.* Name events that are examples of a hot war or a cold war and have students call out "hot" or "cold."

Follow-Up Activities: **1.** Have students use the Cause and Effect graphic organizer on page 111 of this guide to show the two main ways the United States worked to stop the spread of communism. **2.** Help students use the Geography Theme: Movement blackline master on page 118 of this guide to explain the spread of communism during the Cold War. Students should use information in this chapter as well as any outside resources to complete this activity. **3.** Help students use the Geography Theme: Place blackline master on page 116 of this guide to describe Berlin, Germany. Students should use information in this chapter as well as any outside resources to complete this activity.

Chapter Online Resources:
Find more information about topics in this chapter at *www.HarcourtAchieve.com/AchievementZone.* Click on *America's Story.*

ANSWER KEY

Learning From Pictures (Bk 2, p. 100; CE, p. 244)
Answers will vary, but should include that it was meant to prevent the people of Communist East Berlin from trying to move to West Berlin.

Using What You've Learned

Match Up (Bk 2, p. 104; CE, p. 248)
1. e   **2.** c   **3.** a   **4.** d   **5.** b

Understanding Different Points of View
(Bk 2, p. 104; CE, p. 248)
1. Soviet   **2.** American   **3.** American   **4.** Soviet
5. Soviet   **6.** American   **7.** American   **8.** Soviet

Reading a Historical Map (Bk 2, p. 105; CE, p. 249)
1. the Soviet Union   **2.** France and Italy   **3.** neutral

Journal Writing (Bk 2, p. 105; CE, p. 249)
Answers will vary. Paragraphs should include that in a democracy people vote for their leaders and have many freedoms. In a Communist government, the government owns most land, stores, and businesses; the country is ruled by a dictator; and people do not have freedom of speech or religion.

TEACHING STRATEGIES

Summary: Life improved for many Americans. Doctors found vaccines to prevent polio. Americans feared the spread of communism. The Supreme Court ruled against segregation in schools.

Objective: Students will understand the advances and decisions that helped improve American life during the 1950s. They will also understand the new kinds of problems that faced the people of the United States.

Pre-Reading Activities: 1. Ask students to identify some of the vaccines they have received to prevent disease. Tell them that in this chapter they will learn about the discovery of two polio vaccines. **2.** Have students review the meaning of segregation and the laws written in the South after the Civil War that allowed segregation. Tell students that they will learn about segregation in the United States after World War II.

Vocabulary Activities: Discuss the meaning of each of the vocabulary words. Call on students to use the words in oral sentences.

Review Words
(Bk 2, Chaps. 1–15; CE, Chaps. 22–36) weapons, Cold War, atomic bomb, communism, Great Depression, segregation
(Bk 1 and CE, Chaps. 1–21) invented, goods, Senate, senators, Supreme Court, Constitution, justices, general

Post-Reading Discussion Points: 1. Discuss how American life improved during the 1950s. Ask students how the G.I. Bill of Rights and the Supreme Court decision *Brown* v. *Board of Education of Topeka, Kansas* helped improve the lives of Americans. **2.** Ask students how Jonas Salk and Albert Sabin's work was important. **3.** Read and discuss excerpts from Margaret Chase Smith's "Declaration of Conscience" speech in which she spoke out against Senator Joseph McCarthy.

ELL Activity: Show students photos from books, magazines, or newspapers of the United States in the 1950s. Ask students to write a few sentences explaining how the United States is similar or different today.

Follow-Up Activities: 1. Have students use the Concept Web graphic organizer on page 109 of this guide to show the major events during the 1950s. Have students use the completed Concept Webs to write summaries of the events in the chapter. **2.** Encourage students to research and report on one of the people listed in People & Places in this chapter.

Chapter Online Resources:
Find more information about topics in this chapter at *www.HarcourtAchieve.com/AchievementZone*. Click on *America's Story*.

ANSWER KEY

Learning From Pictures (Bk 2, p. 106; CE, p. 250) Answers will vary, but should include that times were better after World War II, many families could afford to own homes, a car, and there was more room for children to play.

Using What You've Learned

Who Am I? (Bk 2, p. 109; CE, p. 253)
1. Harry S Truman **2.** Dwight D. Eisenhower **3.** Jonas Salk **4.** Joseph McCarthy **5.** Margaret Chase Smith **6.** Thurgood Marshall

Fact or Opinion (Bk 2, p. 109; CE, p. 253)
1. F **2.** F **3.** F **4.** O **5.** F **6.** O **(CE) 7.** F **(CE) 8.** F **(CE) 9.** O

Comparing Circle Graphs (Bk 2, p. 110; CE, p. 254)
1. 74 **2.** 26 **3.** suburbs **4.** faster

Journal Writing (Bk 2, p. 110; CE, p. 254) Answers will vary. Students should tell about two ways life improved for many Americans. Answers might include the following: Korean War ended; a huge system of highways was started; space was explored; many babies were born; G.I. Bill of Rights was passed; polio vaccines were discovered; Americans had many consumer goods to buy; Supreme Court decision in *Brown* v. *Board of Education of Topeka, Kansas* helped end segregation laws.

TEACHING STRATEGIES

Summary: Martin Luther King, Jr., led a movement for civil rights for all Americans.

Objective: Students will understand how Martin Luther King, Jr., used peaceful means to change laws that affected African Americans and all other Americans.

Pre-Reading Activities: **1.** Invite someone who attended the 1963 "March on Washington" to speak to the class about the event. Tell students that this event was an important part of the civil rights movement. **2.** Ask students to discuss how peaceful methods can create change.

Vocabulary Activities: **1.** Have students explain the difference between a strike and a boycott. **2.** Ask students to use the chapter pictures to help them write sentences using the new words.

Review Words
(Bk 2, Chaps. 1–16; CE, Chaps. 22–37) segregation, reporter, equal rights, arrested
(Bk 1 and CE, Chaps. 1–21) Civil War, Supreme Court, Constitution, Congress, nation, citizens

Post-Reading Discussion Points: **1.** Point out that many different groups of Americans did not like the laws that kept African Americans from having equal rights. **2.** Ask students to discuss how a boycott can change people's attitudes by causing economic hardship. Have students use the Montgomery bus boycott to show how such an action can bring hardship to both sides. **3.** Ask students to explain how the Civil Rights Act of 1964 helped Americans.

Primary Source Quote: 1. This quote is from *Quiet Strength* by Rosa Parks. In it she recalls her contribution to the American civil rights movement. **2.** This quote is from King's famous "I Have a Dream" speech in which he spoke about the hopes of equal opportunity and treatment for all Americans.

ELL Activity: Have students locate and label sites of events in the civil rights movement on a wall map, giving the date and a description of the event.

Primary Source Activities: **1.** Ask students to discuss the actions of Rosa Parks and the effects of those actions. Discuss how reading about the event in Rosa Parks' own words is different than reading about the event in a book written by a person who was not there. **2.** Read students excerpts from Martin Luther King, Jr.'s, "I Have a Dream" speech or have students listen to a recording or view a video of the speech. Discuss the main ideas in the speech as well as the tone of delivery.

Follow-Up Activities: **1.** Have students research and report on Lyndon B. Johnson's participation in the civil rights movement.

Chapter Online Resources:
Find more information about topics in this chapter at *www.HarcourtAchieve.com/AchievementZone.* Click on *America's Story.*

ANSWER KEY

Learning From Pictures (Bk 2, p. 112; CE, p. 256) fingerprinting Rosa Parks
(Bk 2, p. 114; CE, p. 258) Answers will vary, but should include that they supported civil rights and wanted to hear what King had to say.

Using Primary Sources (Bk 2, p. 115; CE, p. 259)
1. They paid at the front door, got off the bus, and then reentered through the back door. **2.** to go home **3.** because she did not give up her seat on the bus to a white passenger **4.** because she could have been treated very badly by the police **5. Constructed Response:** equal justice for all citizens

Using What You've Learned

Choose a Word (Bk 2, p. 116; CE, p. 260)
1. Rosa Parks **2.** Birmingham **3.** northern **4.** Washington **5.** Civil Rights **(CE) 6.** Nobel

Using Graphic Organizers: Main Idea and Supporting Details (Bk 2, p. 116; CE, p. 260)
1. King and other leaders tried to change laws peacefully. **2.** African Americans in Montgomery started a bus boycott to change an unfair bus law.

TEACHING STRATEGIES

Summary: Americans traveled to the moon in 1969. Americans have developed satellites and space shuttles to study space and Earth.

Objective: Students will learn about the major developments in space exploration since the space race first began in 1957.

Pre-Reading Activities: 1. After looking at the chapter photographs, ask students to describe the outfits worn by the astronauts and the vehicles used to go into space. **2.** Ask students if they have ever imagined traveling in space.

Vocabulary Activities: 1. Have students write sentences with each of the new words. **2.** Ask students if they know any other uses for the word *shuttle.* Have them explain why they think the space shuttle has this name.

Review Words
(Bk 2, Chaps. 1–17; CE, Chaps. 22–38)
    Cold War
(Bk 1 and CE, Chaps. 1–21) invented, nation

Post-Reading Discussion Points: 1. Ask students to discuss whether space travel would have taken longer if there had not been a space race. **2.** Ask students to discuss why the most powerful nations would want to control space, especially during the Cold War.

Primary Source Quote: At 4:18 P.M. EST, four days after *Apollo 11* took off from Earth, it touched down on the moon.

ELL Activity: Have students pairs use the textbook and other resources to learn about the United States space program. Then have pairs tell what they have learned.

Geography Theme Activities: Have students browse the National Aeronautics and Space Administration website at www.nasa.gov to find the list of United States space facilities. On a map of the United States, have students find the locations of these sites. Point out to students that most of the space facilities are located near the Atlantic or Pacific oceans.

Follow-Up Activities: 1. Have students write to NASA in Houston, Texas, to obtain information and photographs about the most recent space shuttle flights. The phone number for the Johnson Space

Center's Media Resource Center is (281) 483-0123. **2.** Have students use the Sequencing graphic organizer on page 110 of this guide to show how space exploration has developed.

Chapter Online Resources:
Find more information about topics in this chapter at *www.HarcourtAchieve.com/AchievementZone.* Click on *America's Story.*

ANSWER KEY

Learning From Pictures (Bk 2, p. 117; CE, p. 261) to show that the United States was the first country to reach the moon

Using Geography Themes (Bk 2, p. 121; CE, p. 265)
1. It had few people, was near the ocean so spaceships could land safely in the water, and did not get snow. **2.** Merritt Island **3.** 47 miles **4.** the Banana River **5.** north **6.** Answers will vary. Students should give two ways to describe where the Kennedy Space Center is located using directions or what is near or around it.

Using What You've Learned

Write the Answer (Bk 2, p. 122; CE, p. 266)
1. The Soviet Union sent the world's first satellite into space in 1957. The next year the United States sent their first satellite into space. **2.** Kennedy said the United States would send people to the moon by 1970. **3.** *Apollo 11* took the first Americans to the moon. **4.** The first three astronauts to fly to the moon were Neil Armstrong, Edwin Aldrin, and Michael Collins. **5.** It can be used many times. **(CE) 6.** The *Challenger* suddenly blew up, and all seven Americans inside were killed. **(CE) 7.** She became the first woman to command a space shuttle flight. **(CE) 8.** Ellen Ochoa helped bring important supplies to the space station in 1999. **(CE) 9.** The rovers collected rocks from Mars.

Categories (Bk 2, p. 122; CE, p. 266)
1. Space Race **2.** Satellite **3.** Space Shuttle **4.** International Space Station

Reading a Line Graph (Bk 2, p. 123; CE, p. 267)
1. 22 **2.** 33 **3.** *Apollo 17* **4.** more

Journal Writing (Bk 2, p. 123; CE, p. 267)
Answers will vary. Students should explain Neil Armstrong's statement, "That's one small step for (a) man; one giant leap for mankind."

TEACHING STRATEGIES

Summary: César Chávez and Dolores Huerta worked to help migrant farm workers get better pay and safer working conditions.

Objective: Students will understand the goals and methods of César Chávez and the United Farm Workers to help migrant farm workers.

Pre-Reading Activities: 1. Have students describe the chapter illustrations. Based on these pictures, what do students think the chapter will be about? **2.** Review the peaceful methods that Martin Luther King, Jr., used to get unfair laws changed in America. Tell students that César Chávez was influenced by the work of Martin Luther King, Jr.

Vocabulary Activities: 1. Help students use the dictionary to learn the etymology of the word *pesticide.* **2.** Have students write sentences using each vocabulary word.

Review Words
(Bk 2, Chaps. 1–18; CE, Chaps. 22–39) strike, boycott, labor unions, salaries, Great Depression
(Bk 1 and CE, Chaps. 1–21) crops

Post-Reading Discussion Points: 1. Ask students to compare Chávez's methods to help migrant farm workers with the methods Martin Luther King, Jr., used to help African Americans. **2.** Have students review how unions helped America's factory workers. Ask students to explain how unions also helped migrant farm workers. **3.** Ask students to explain why many storeowners refused to sell grapes during the grape boycott.

Primary Source Quote: Arturo Rodriguez spoke these words before a crowd of more than1,500 people during César Chávez Day in Los Angeles on August 18, 2000.

ELL Activity: Display labeled pictures of people and events from this chapter and refer to them often. When students are familiar with the chapter material, give each student a picture. Have students ask each other *yes* or *no* questions in order to find out which picture they have.

Follow-Up Activities: 1. Invite students to learn more about the hazards of pesticides and herbicides used in agriculture. Have students discuss the need for safety precautions when using these products. **2.** Have students write *César Chávez Helps the Farm Workers* in the center of the Concept Web graphic organizer found on page 109 of this guide. Have students write on the spokes ways that César Chávez helped the farm workers. Ask students to write a summary based on the information in the web.

Chapter Online Resources:
Find more information about topics in this chapter at *www.HarcourtAchieve.com/AchievementZone.* Click on *America's Story.*

ANSWER KEY

Learning From Pictures (Bk 2, p. 125; CE, p. 269)
picking grapes

Using What You've Learned

Choose the Answer (Bk 2, p. 127; CE, p. 271)
1. migrant farm workers **2.** Dolores Huerta **3.** went on strike **4.** grapes **5.** contracts

Sequencing Events (Bk 2, p. 127; CE, p. 271)
The sentences should be in the following order:
(Bk 2) 5, 3, 4, 2, 1. **(CE) 1.** As a child, César Chávez went to 37 different schools. **2.** César Chávez started the United Farm Workers in 1962. **3.** In 1965 César Chávez led a strike and a boycott against the grape growers. **4.** César Chávez died in 1993. **5.** Arturo Rodriguez now leads the United Farm Workers.

Journal Writing (Bk 2, p. 127; CE, p. 271)
Answers will vary. Paragraphs should acknowledge the need for contracts and better salaries and that pesticides should not be used.

Using a Map Key to Read a Resource Map
(Bk 2, p. 128; CE, p. 272)
1. grapes **2.** lettuce **3.** rice **(CE) 4.** near Sacramento

TEACHING STRATEGIES

Summary: Americans fought unsuccessfully against the spread of communism in Vietnam. Americans were deeply divided about whether to support this war.

Objective: Students will understand the reasons for United States involvement in Vietnam and why Americans did not agree on whether or not to support the Vietnam War.

Pre-Reading Activities: 1. Using the world map on page 124 of this guide, have students draw and label the United States, North Korea, South Korea, North Vietnam, South Vietnam, the Soviet Union, and China. **2.** Ask students how a jungle climate with thick forests and very hot weather might make it more difficult to fight in a war. **3.** Ask students what they might do if they believed very strongly that America was doing something wrong.

Vocabulary Activities: 1. Help students use a dictionary to learn the etymology of *cease-fire* and *memorial*. **2.** Call on students to use each of the new words in an oral sentence.

Review Words
(Bk 2, Chaps. 1–19; CE, Chaps. 22–40)
   communism, election, Cold War, spread of
   communism, weapons, immigrants, protest
(Bk 1 and CE, Chaps. 1–21) nation, captured,
   surrendered, goal

Post-Reading Discussion Points: 1. Ask students if they think the United States was right to try to stop the spread of communism in other parts of the world. Help students identify the pros and cons of United States involvement in Vietnam. **2.** Discuss how television during the Vietnam War might have influenced people's opinions.

Primary Source Quote: Maya Lin designed the Vietnam Veterans Memorial at age 21.

ELL Activity: Discuss how American soldiers in Vietnam might have felt about the antiwar protests.

Follow-Up Activities: 1. Have students research reasons for the American involvement in Vietnam. **2.** Have students use the Event Description graphic organizer on page 114 of this guide to show important information about the Vietnam War. In the center box, have students write *Vietnam War.* Students should complete the rest of the organizer with information from this chapter. **3.** Have students use the Geography Theme: Region blackline master on page 120 of this guide to tell about the region of South Vietnam. Have students use the map and information in the chapter, as well as any outside resources, to help them complete the activity.

Chapter Online Resources:
Find more information about topics in this chapter at *www.HarcourtAchieve.com/AchievementZone.* Click on *America's Story.*

ANSWER KEY

Using Maps (Bk 2, p. 130; CE, p. 274)
Hanoi and Saigon

Learning From Pictures (Bk 2, p.132; CE, p. 276)
to honor and remember the people who died in the Vietnam War

Using What You've Learned

Finish the Sentence (Bk 2, p. 133; CE, p. 277)
1. Southeast **2.** Vietnam **3.** Viet Cong **4.** Nixon
5. thousand

Cause and Effect (Bk 2, p. 133; CE, p. 277)
1. d **2.** a **3.** c **4.** b

Reading a Bar Graph (Bk 2, p. 134; CE, p. 278)
1. 1968 **2.** 1967, 1968, and 1969 **3.** 1969
(CE) 4. 1972

Journal Writing (Bk 2, p. 134; CE, p. 278)
Answers will vary. Paragraphs might include that protesters believed that too many American soldiers were being killed, that it cost too much money to fight in Vietnam, and that the money should be spent in the United States.

Name _____

◄ UNIT REVIEW ►

OUR CHANGING NATION

Choose the Answer   Use the time line from the unit opener to answer the questions below. Draw a circle around the correct answer.

1. When did American soldiers begin fighting in Vietnam?
   1950   1965   1975

2. Which event happened first?
   The Korean War ended.
   Martin Luther King, Jr., led the March on Washington.
   The Berlin Wall was torn down.

3. Who won the first contract for migrant farm workers?
   Martin Luther King, Jr.   Eileen Collins   César Chávez

4. In what year did South Vietnam surrender to North Vietnam?
   1975   1961   1953

Match Up   Finish each sentence in Group A with words from Group B. Write the letter of the correct answer on the blank line.

Group A

1. The law that made it easy for veterans to get loans was the _____ .

2. The first woman to command a space shuttle flight was _____ .

3. The _____ is an organization that works for world peace.

4. In 1964 Congress passed the _____ , giving equal rights to all Americans.

5. People in South Vietnam who fought against the government were called the _____ .

Group B

a. United Nations

b. Civil Rights Act

c. G.I. Bill of Rights

d. Viet Cong

e. Eileen Collins

Name _____

◄ UNIT REVIEW ►

OUR CHANGING NATION

Riddle Review Use a word in dark print to complete each sentence below. Write the word on the blanks next to each sentence.

school	**bus**	**McCarthy**	**spray**
Cold	**moon**	**protests**	

1. Rosa Parks refused to go to the back of the _____ .
   □ __ __

2. Martin Luther King, Jr., wanted African American and white children to go to _____ together.
   __ __ __ __ □ __ __

3. Many farmers _____ their grapes with pesticides.
   __ __ __ __ __ □

4. The Soviet Union and the United States fought the _____ War without guns.
   □ __ __ __

5. Neil Armstrong and Edwin Aldrin were the first people to walk on the _____ .
   __ __ □ __

6. Many Americans held _____ against the war in Vietnam.
   __ __ __ □ __ __ __

7. Senator Margaret Chase Smith spoke out against Senator _____ in the United States Senate.
   __ __ __ __ __ □ __ __

The letters in the boxes spell a word. The word answers a riddle.

RIDDLE: What did people do to help the grape pickers?

ANSWER: __ __ __ __ __ __ __

Name _____

◁ UNIT TEST ▷
OUR CHANGING NATION

True or False   Write **T** next to each sentence that is true. Write **F** next to each sentence that is false.

_____ 1. In 1975 North Vietnam surrendered to South Vietnam.

_____ 2. César Chávez helped the grape pickers get contracts and safer working conditions.

_____ 3. All seven astronauts inside the *Challenger* were killed when their space shuttle exploded.

_____ 4. Martin Luther King, Jr., worked to get African Americans more rights.

_____ 5. The Cold War became a real war in Korea.

_____ 6. The United States had a baby boom after World War II.

Match Up   Finish each sentence in Group A with words from Group B. Write the letter of the correct answer on the blank line.

Group A

1. Martin Luther King, Jr., was given the _____ .

2. César Chávez started the _____ .

3. The United States sent the first people to the moon in the _____ spaceship.

4. News reports on television showed how hard it was for soldiers to fight in _____ .

5. _____ made the first polio vaccine.

Group B

a. *Apollo 11*

b. Nobel Peace Prize

c. United Farm Workers

d. Jonas Salk

e. Vietnam

Name _____

◁ UNIT TEST ▷

OUR CHANGING NATION

Sequencing Events   Write the numbers **1**, **2**, **3**, **4**, and **5** next to these sentences to show the correct order.

_____   The Berlin Wall was torn down.

_____   In 1961 the Soviet Union built a wall to separate East Berlin and West Berlin.

_____   In 1970 most California grape growers gave contracts to the grape pickers.

_____   Many Americans marched in large cities to protest the Vietnam War.

_____   In 1955 African Americans decided to boycott the buses in Montgomery.

Finish the Sentence   Draw a circle around the word or words that finish each sentence.

1. The Supreme Court case called *Brown* v. *Board of Education of Topeka, Kansas* helped end _____ laws.
   Communist   veteran   segregation

2. The armies of _____ nations have promised to help one another in a war.
   Teamsters   NATO   Cold War

3. Some Americans believed America should not fight in Vietnam because _____ .
   Japan needed more help
   too many American soldiers were being killed
   the weather was very cold in Vietnam

4. The _____ became part of the Cold War.
   space shuttle   space race   spaceship

5. _____ said, "I have a dream."
   John F. Kennedy   Martin Luther King, Jr.   César Chávez

6. César Chávez and Dolores Huerta started a union _____ .
   to help migrant farm workers
   to get equal rights for women, African Americans, and veterans
   to tell the United States government not to fight in Vietnam

TEACHING STRATEGIES

Summary: The United States emerged as the strongest world leader at the end of the Cold War. It is working to improve trade, fight pollution, protect natural resources, and attain world peace.

Major Concepts:
- **Economics:** NAFTA and PNTR were created to lower tariffs between the United States and some of its trading partners.
- **History:** NAFTA and the Clean Air Act were created to help relations among the United States and its neighbors.
- **Sociology:** The Americans with Disabilities Act was passed to help people with disabilities have equal rights. Technology has changed communication around the world. Americans are working to solve pollution problems.

Pre-Reading Activities: **1.** Have students bring to class newspaper and magazine clippings about pollution, the depletion of natural resources, or acid rain. **2.** Have students gather news items that deal with relations between the United States and other countries, especially Canada, Mexico, and Russia. **3.** Have students discuss ways their lives today differ from their parents' lives thirty years ago as a result of technology.

Post-Reading Discussion Points: **1.** Ask students whether they think the United States should help countries around the world solve their problems. Have students explain their responses. **2.** Ask students to discuss the importance of technology in the world today. How has it improved communication? **3.** Have students discuss the environmental issues presented in this unit.

Follow-Up Activities: **1.** Ask students to discuss how the United States is trying to solve environmental, economic, and social problems. **2.** Have students use the Sequencing graphic organizer on page 110 of this guide to show how the United States has worked for world peace since the Cold War.

Review Activities: Refer to pages 101–102 of this guide for review activities covering this unit. Refer to page 105 for a time line review covering Bk 2, Units 1–5/CE, Units 5–9.

Assessment: Refer to pages 103–104 of this guide for the Unit Test. Refer to pages 106–107 for the Final Test covering Bk 2, Units 1–5/CE, Units 5–9.

ANSWER KEY

Unit Review (Bk 2, p. 158; CE, p. 315)
1. disabilities **2.** Cold War **3.** NAFTA **4.** China
5. Pentagon **6.** Saddam Hussein **7.** medicine
8. George W. Bush

Unit Review (Teacher's Guide, pp. 101–102)

Choose the Answer 1. The Berlin Wall was torn down. **2.** Mexico **3.** 1990 **4.** Bosnia and Kosovo

Match Up 1. e **2.** d **3.** b **4.** c **5.** a

Riddle Review 1. chips **2.** rain **3.** NAFTA
4. aliens **5.** Iraq **6.** PNTR **7.** cell **8.** control
Answer: I N T E R N E T

Unit Test (Teacher's Guide, pp. 103–104)

True or False 1. F **2.** T **3.** T **4.** F **5.** T **6.** T

Match Up 1. c **2.** a **3.** d **4.** b **5.** e

Sequencing Events The sentences should be numbered 1, 4, 2, 3, 5.

Finish the Sentence 1. French **2.** pollution
3. natural resources **4.** Kuwait **5.** Russia

Time Line Review covering Bk 2, Units 1–5/CE, Units 5–9 (Teacher's Guide, p. 105)
The correct order, top to bottom, is c, l, b, d, f, e, h, j, i, a, g, k.

Final Test covering Bk 2, Units 1–5/CE, Units 5–9 (Teacher's Guide, pp. 106–107)

True or False 1. T **2.** T **3.** T **4.** T **5.** F **6.** T

Match Up 1. d **2.** a **3.** c **4.** b **5.** e

Sequencing Events The sentences should be numbered 1, 4, 5, 2, 3.

Finish the Sentence 1. imperialism
2. Reconstruction **3.** Germany **4.** vote
5. NAACP **6.** the Vietnam War

TEACHING STRATEGIES

Summary: America is working to solve problems and to improve trade with its neighbors.

Objective: Students will understand how the friendship of the United States with its neighbors has led to anti–pollution laws and increased trade.

Pre-Reading Activities: 1. Ask students who have been to Canada or Mexico to describe their experiences or show photographs. **2.** Discuss the importance of good relations with neighbors.

Vocabulary Activities: 1. Have students use a dictionary to find meanings of the words *unguarded* and *illegal.* Ask students to think of other words that begin with *un-* or *il-* to determine the meanings of these prefixes. **2.** Have students write sentences using each of the new words.

Review Words
(Bk 2, Chaps. 1–20; CE, Chaps. 22–41) democracy, salaries, industry
(Bk 1 and CE, Chaps. 1–21) nation, capital, tax, Congress, tariffs, goods, in debt, environment, crops

Post-Reading Discussion Points: 1. Discuss how the economies of the United States, Mexico, and Canada are closely linked. **2.** Have students discuss the positive and negative effects of NAFTA on the United States, Canada, and Mexico.

Primary Source Quote: This quote is from a speech made by President Bill Clinton during a meeting of newspaper editors on April 11, 1997.

ELL Activity: Have students identify an environmental problem in their school or community. Help students create a plan for solving one problem and set individual and class goals to achieve a solution.

Geography Theme Activities: 1. Invite students to learn more about areas of the world hurt by acid rain. Have them report their findings to the class. **2.** Ask students to think of ways they can help decrease air pollution.

Follow-Up Activities: 1. Using outside resources, have students use the Geography Theme: Place blackline master on page 116 of this guide to describe Canada or Mexico.

Chapter Online Resources:
Find more information about topics in this chapter at *www.HarcourtAchieve.com/AchievementZone.* Click on *America's Story.*

ANSWER KEY

Using Maps (Bk 2, p. 139; CE, p. 283)
St. Lawrence Seaway

Learning From Pictures (Bk 2, p. 141; CE, p. 285)
by truck

Using Geography Themes (Bk 2, p. 143; CE, p. 287)
1. It kills trees, farm crops, and other plants. It also hurts fish and plants when it falls into lakes and rivers. **2.** Pollution is sent into the air; rain becomes acid rain. **3.** Winds blow the Northeast's air pollution into eastern Canada. **4.** They are making laws to control air pollution and trying different ways to make energy. **5.** by turning off lights and televisions to save electricity and by walking or riding a bike to use less gasoline **6.** Students should list two of the following cities with acid rain: Montréal, Toronto, Boston, New York City.

Using What You've Learned

Choose a Word (Bk 2, p. 144; CE, p. 288)
1. Quebec **2.** Clean Air Act **3.** oil **4.** NAFTA **5.** tariffs

Using Graphic Organizers: Main Idea and Supporting Details (Bk 2, p. 144; CE, p. 288)
1. There is friendship between the United States and Canada.
2. The United States trades with its neighbors in Latin America.

Reading a Double Line Graph (Bk 2, p. 145; CE, p. 289)
1. 1994 **2.** 2003 **3.** 85 billion **4.** grew larger

TEACHING STRATEGIES

Summary: Since the end of the Cold War in 1991, the United States has worked toward world peace.

Objective: Students will understand the changes that have occurred since the Cold War and how the United States works toward peace in countries around the world.

Pre-Reading Activities: 1. Review with students the causes and the events of the Cold War. Ask students how they think the Cold War ended. **2.** Have students use a wall map to identify the former Soviet Union and the fifteen countries that became independent in 1991. **3.** Have students locate on a world map Kuwait, Iraq, the Persian Gulf, Israel, Jordan, Egypt, Bosnia, Serbia, and Kosovo. Explain that these are places that they will learn about in this chapter.

Vocabulary Activities: 1. Discuss the meanings of the new words. **2.** Review the meaning of acronyms and remind students of previous acronyms such as NATO and NAFTA.

Review Words
(Bk 2, Chaps. 1–21; CE, Chaps. 22–42)
   Cold War, United Nations, NATO, weapons, democracy, communism
(Bk 1 and CE, Chaps. 1–21) nation, capital, independent, goal, destroyed, religions, peace treaty, tariffs

Post-Reading Discussion Points: 1. Have students review the differences between a democracy and a Communist government. Ask students what changes might have to occur if a Communist government becomes a democracy. **2.** Ask students why they think America helped Kuwait become free from Iraq's control. Have students explain their ideas. **3.** Have students discuss the goal and the methods of the United States to achieve world peace. **4.** Show students photographs of soldiers in camouflage from the Vietnam War and the Persian Gulf War. Ask students why soldiers might be dressed so differently in the two wars.

ELL Activity: Write the names of countries mentioned in the chapter on slips of paper. Have students take turns drawing names. Have them identify one way that the country drawn is linked to the United States in this chapter.

Follow-Up Activities: 1. Have students research the reasons for America's involvement in the Persian Gulf War. **2.** Have students use the Concept Web graphic organizer on page 109 of this guide to list ways that the United States has worked toward world peace. Ask them to write a summary based on the web. **3.** Have students use the Geography Theme: Location blackline master on page 117 of this guide to describe the location of Kuwait. Tell students to use the map in this chapter as well as any outside resources to help them complete this activity.

Chapter Online Resources:
Find more information about topics in this chapter at *www.HarcourtAchieve.com/AchievementZone.* Click on *America's Story.*

ANSWER KEY

Using Maps (Bk 2, p. 148; CE, p. 292)
Serbia and Croatia

Learning From Pictures (Bk 2, p. 149; CE, p. 293)
by delivering food

Using What You've Learned

True or False (Bk 2, p. 150; CE, p. 294)
1. T **2.** F **3.** T **4.** T **5.** F **6.** T

Cause and Effect (Bk 2, p. 150; CE, p. 294)
1. d **2.** a **3.** b **4.** e **5.** c

Reading a Double Bar Graph (Bk 2, p. 151; CE, p. 295)
1. $100 billion **2.** 2003 **3.** $25 billion **4.** 2003
5. 2000

TEACHING STRATEGIES

Summary: Technology has changed the way America communicates. The United States is working to protect its environment.

Objective: Students will understand some of the changes and challenges that the United States has faced.

Pre-Reading Activities: **1.** Ask students how they would feel if they were not given a job because of a disability. **2.** Ask students whether they have used a cell phone, fax machine, or the Internet. **3.** Ask students how they use energy each day. Then ask if they try to save energy or recycle at home.

Vocabulary Activities: Help students create a word map linking the vocabulary terms. They could begin with *technology* and create a concept web or a chain. Ask them to explain the relationships they see between the various terms.

Review Words
(Bk 2, Chaps. 1–22; CE, Chaps. 22–43) immigrants, equal rights, democracy, Civil Rights Act of 1964, natural resources, pollution, fossil fuels, acid rain, election
(Bk 1 and CE, Chaps. 1–21) Congress, senators, nation, disabilities, Constitution

Post-Reading Discussion Points: **1.** Ask students to list some of the changes and problems that America has faced. **2.** Discuss ways that natural resources are being destroyed. What can be done to prevent such destruction? **3.** Have students list as many examples of technology as they can.

Primary Source Quote: Carleton Fiorina rose from modest beginnings to become an important business leader. She frequently gives speeches around the country about what technology can offer communities.

ELL Activity: Have students create collages, illustrations, stories, essays, or other creative works showing new technology discussed in the chapter. Then have students present their work to the class.

Follow-Up Activities: **1.** Ask students to try to live one day without using technology and keep a diary of their experiences. **2.** Have students use the Concept Web graphic organizer on page 109 of this guide to show ways people can save energy or natural resources. **3.** Invite students to initiate a recycling

or energy saving program at home. Then ask them to write a paper describing the experience. **4.** Have students use the Geography Theme: Human/Environment Interaction blackline master on page 119 of this guide to describe how the United States is using its natural resources. Tell students to use the information in this chapter as well as outside resources to help them complete this activity.

Chapter Online Resources:
Find more information about topics in this chapter at *www.HarcourtAchieve.com/AchievementZone*. Click on *America's Story*.

ANSWER KEY

Learning From Pictures (Bk 2, p. 154; CE, p. 298)
a computer

Using What You've Learned

Match Up (Bk 2, p. 156; CE, p. 300)
1. b **2.** a **3.** d **4.** c

Categories (Bk 2, p. 156; CE, p. 300)
1. Ways to Make Energy **2.** Recycling
3. Technology **4.** Global Warming

Journal Writing (Bk 2, p. 156; CE, p. 300)
Answers will vary. Letters should identify a specific problem and suggest at least one solution to that problem.

Writing an Outline (Bk 2, p. 157; CE, p. 301)
1. A Changing Nation **2.** Changing People, Problems in Our Nation, New Technologies **3.** Computers and the Internet, Camera phones, Human genes and DNA **(CE) 4.** Problems in Our Nation **5.** Answers may vary. Students should point out that writing an outline can help organize ideas in a chapter.

TEACHING STRATEGIES

Summary: Terrorism became a new concern for Americans in the 21st century. Through attacks on countries that harbored terrorists, the Patriot Act of 2001, and the Department of Homeland Security, the United States is working towards ending terrorism.

Objective: Students will understand how the United States is working to end terrorism.

Pre-Reading Activities: **1.** Have students study the Primary Source quote in this chapter. Ask students to discuss how respecting the beliefs of others can make the world safer. **2.** Ask students what it would be like if the world had no weapons of mass destruction.

Vocabulary Activities: **1.** Discuss the meanings of the new words. **2.** Ask students to use the pictures in the chapter to help them write sentences using the new words.

Review Words
(Bk 2, Chaps. 1–23; CE, Chaps. 22–44) United Nations, Persian Gulf War, cell phones
(Bk 1 and CE, Chaps. 1–22) freedom of religion, Congress, Supreme Court

Post-Reading Discussion Points: **1.** Ask students to list some of the problems the United States has begun to face in the 21st century. **2.** Ask students to discuss how the Patriot Act of 2001 can help keep Americans safe. **3.** Ask students to discuss why the Iraq War began.

Primary Source Quote: Rudy Giuliani spoke these words to the United Nations General Assembly on October 1, 2001.

ELL Activity: Ask students to look at a map Europe. Point out America's allies in the Iraq War—Britain, Spain, and Italy—on the map. Have volunteers tell what they know about these countries. Divide students into groups. Assign each group a country. Have each group write questions about what they would like to learn about their country. Encourage students to do research to find answers to their questions.

Follow-Up Activities: **1.** Have students use the Sequencing graphic organizer on page 110 of this guide to show the sequence of events that led the United States into a war with Iraq. **2.** Have students use the Geography Theme: Place blackline master on page 116 of this guide to describe countries in Central Asia and the Middle East. **3.** Discuss the purpose of the

Department of Homeland Security. Ask students how they think it might keep America safe from terrorism.

Chapter Online Resources:
Find more information about topics in this chapter at *www.HarcourtAchieve.com/AchievementZone.* Click on *America's Story.*

ANSWER KEY

Learning From Pictures (Bk 2, p. 159, CE, p. 303) raising the American flag

Using Maps (Bk 2, p. 161; CE, p. 305)
Syria, Turkey, Iran, Kuwait, Saudi Arabia, Jordan

Write the Answer (Bk 2, p. 163; CE, p. 307)
1. Al Gore and George W. Bush received almost the same number of votes. It took more than five weeks to decide who would be President. The United States Supreme Court made a decision that allowed George W. Bush to win the election. **2.** On September 11, 2001 two planes crashed into the Twin Towers, a third plane crashed into the Pentagon, and the fourth plane crashed in a field in Pennsylvania. **3.** Osama bin Laden is the leader of al Qaeda. **4.** Bin Laden hates freedom of religion and wants to destroy America and its friends. **5.** The American army attacked Afghanistan and defeated the Taliban. Americans helped start a new government that allowed more freedom. **(CE) 6.** The job of the Department of Homeland Security is to stop terrorism. **(CE) 7.** Saddam Hussein was the ruler of Iraq. American soldiers captured him in December 2003. **(CE) 8.** Iraq refused to tell what had happened to all of the weapons of mass destruction it had.

Sequencing Events (Bk 2, p. 163; CE, p. 307)
The sentences should be in the following order:
(Bk 2) 2, 3, 5, 4, 1. **(CE) 1.** Saddam Hussein ruled Iraq after the Persian Gulf War ended in 1991. **2.** In January 2001 George W. Bush became the forty-third President of the United States. **3.** Terrorists hijacked four planes and attacked the United States on September 11, 2001. **4.** Congress passed the Patriot Act in 2001. **5.** Iraqi leaders took control of their government on June 28, 2004.

Journal Writing (Bk 2, p. 163; CE, p. 307)
Answers will vary. Paragraphs should give details about the terrorist attacks on the United States and how students felt about those attacks.

Reading A Newspaper (Bk 2, p. 164; CE, p. 308)
1. June 28, 2004 2. Iraqi Leaders in Control of Government **3.** page 2 **(CE) 4.** page 37
(CE) 5. weather

CHAPTER 46

TEACHING STRATEGIES

Summary: Social Security, Medicare, health insurance, and education are important concerns for America's growing and diverse population.

Objective: Students will recognize the contributions of America's immigrants. They will also understand the problems Americans face with Social Security, Medicare, health insurance, and education and what the government is trying to do to remedy these problems.

Pre-Reading Activities: 1. Discuss why health insurance is important for all Americans. **2.** Have students think about how people pay for the things they need. Then ask students if they know anyone who is retired. Ask students to think about how retired Americans pay for the things they need. Tell students that in this chapter they will learn about how people who are retired pay for the things they need.

Vocabulary Activities: 1. Help students use the dictionary to learn the different uses of the word *boom.* **2.** Call on students to use each of the new words in an oral sentence.

Review Words
(Bk 2, Chaps. 1–23; CE, Chaps. 22–44) immigrants, natural resources, baby boom
(Bk 1 and CE, Chaps. 1–22) tax, Congress

Post-Reading Discussion Points: 1. Ask students to list some of the problems America is facing and the ways in which the government is trying to solve these problems. **2.** Help students use the Internet to find out more about the contributions immigrants have made to American society.

Primary Source Quote: Senator Kennedy delivered this speech at Boston Latin School on January 8, 2002, where he offered his views on education reform and introduced the President.

ELL Activity: Ask students to draw, find pictures of, or bring in items that are part of their culture. Then have students make a display showing the items to the class.

Primary Source Activities: 1. Review the meaning of the vocabulary words with the students. **2.** Read to students primary source materials by previous presidents of the United States.

Follow-Up Activities: 1. Divide students into two groups. Have each group research views on how to solve the problems America faces with health insurance. Tell each group to choose the solution they believe is the best. Have each group present their solution to the class. Then have the class vote on which solution they feel will work the best and why. **2.** Have students use the Concept Web graphic organizer on page 109 of this guide to summarize the problems America is now facing. In the center, have students write *Problems America Faces.* On the spokes, have students write these problems. Have students use information from this chapter and the previous chapter, "America Since the Year 2000."

Chapter Online Resources:
Find more information about topics in this chapter at *www.HarcourtAchieve.com/AchievementZone.* Click on *America's Story.*

ANSWER KEY

Learning From Pictures (Bk 2, p. 167; CE, p. 311)
taking a test

Using Primary Sources (Bk 2, p. 169; CE, p. 313)
1. The country was attacked on September 11, 2001. **2.** The economy is growing. **3.** He helped reform the schools. **4.** He wants affordable health care for more people. He wants to heal the hurt in some neighborhoods. **5. Constructed Response:** Answers will vary, but should include two or more of President Bush's hopes: America will win the war on terror, spread liberty, stay prosperous, and make the world safer. Students' responses should say what their hopes are and how they are the same or different from President Bush's hopes.

Choose a Word (Bk 2, p. 170; CE, p. 314)
1. diverse **2.** baby boomers **3.** retire **4.** Social Security **5.** health insurance

Categories (Bk 2, p. 170; CE, p. 314)
1. Working for a Better America **2.** Changing Population **3.** No Child Left Behind Law **4.** Protecting Social Security

Journal Writing (Bk 2, p. 170; CE, p. 314)
Answers will vary. Paragraphs should list at least three ways students can work for a better America.

Name _____

◄ UNIT REVIEW ►

CHALLENGES IN TODAY'S WORLD

Choose the Answer   Use the time line from the unit opener to answer the questions below. Draw a circle around the correct answer.

1. What happened before the Cold War ended?
   The Berlin Wall was torn down.
   The United States helped end war in Bosnia.
   The United States improved trade with China and Vietnam.

2. Who signed NAFTA with the United States and Canada in 1993?
   Alaska   Mexico   Berlin

3. In which year was the Americans with Disabilities Act passed?
   1989   1990   1993

4. For which countries did the United States work for peace during the 1990s?
   Mexico and Canada   Bosnia and Kosovo   China and Germany

Match Up   Finish each sentence in Group A with words from Group B. Write the letter of the correct answer on the blank line.

Group A

1. _____ helps people who retire pay for the things they need.

2. A Native American named _____ became a senator in 1992.

3. In 1994 Jordan and _____ signed a peace treaty.

4. The _____ allows Americans to own guns.

5. In the Persian Gulf War, American soldiers fought to help _____ become free again.

Group B

a. Kuwait

b. Israel

c. Constitution

d. Ben Nighthorse Campbell

e. Social Security

Name _____

◄ UNIT REVIEW ►

CHALLENGES IN TODAY'S WORLD

Riddle Review   Use a word in dark print to complete each sentence below. Write the word on the blanks next to each sentence.

cell	PNTR	control	chips
NAFTA	Iraq	aliens	rain

1. Tiny pieces of material that store large amounts of information are called computer _____ .

   __ __ ☐ __ __

2. American pollution causes acid _____ in eastern Canada.

   __ __ __ ☐

3. The United States, Canada, and Mexico signed a trade agreement called _____ .

   __ __ __ ☐ __

4. People who come to the United States without permission are illegal _____ .

   __ __ __ ☐ __

5. The _____ War began in 2003.

   __ ☐ __

6. In 2000, the United States agreed to _____ for China.

   __ ☐ __ __

7. People use _____ phones to make calls from almost anywhere.

   __ ☐ __ __

8. A gun _____ law prevents store owners from selling guns to many people who were once in jail.

   __ __ __ ☐ __ __ __

The letters in the boxes spell a word. The word answers a riddle.

RIDDLE: What allows computers to communicate with one another?

ANSWER: __ __ __ __ __ __ __

Name _____

◁ UNIT TEST ▷

CHALLENGES IN TODAY'S WORLD

True or False Write **T** next to each sentence that is true. Write **F** next to each sentence that is false.

_____ 1. French is the only language of Canada.

_____ 2. Millions of working people do not have enough money to pay for health insurance.

_____ 3. The United States helped Israel and Egypt sign a peace treaty.

_____ 4. Most American women earn more money than men do.

_____ 5. Some Americans use wind power to make electricity.

_____ 6. E-mail allows people to send letters by computer to any part of the world.

Match Up Finish each sentence in Group A with words from Group B. Write the letter of the correct answer on the blank line.

Group A

1. Since 1965 millions of _____ and Latin Americans have come to the United States.

2. _____ has changed the way Americans communicate.

3. American soldiers help NATO protect countries in _____ .

4. Ships travel from the Atlantic Ocean through the Great Lakes on the _____ .

5. Illegal aliens come to the United States without _____ .

Group B

a. Technology

b. St. Lawrence Seaway

c. Asians

d. Western Europe

e. permission

Name _____

◄ UNIT TEST ►
CHALLENGES IN TODAY'S WORLD

Sequencing Events   Write the numbers **1, 2, 3, 4,** and **5** next to these sentences to show the correct order.

_____   In 1990 Congress passed the Americans with Disabilities Act.

_____   The United States gave PNTR to China in order to improve relations with the Communist nation.

_____   The Cold War ended in 1991.

_____   In 1993 the United States, Mexico, and Canada signed NAFTA.

_____   Congress passed a law called "No Child Left Behind."

Finish the Sentence   Draw a circle around the word or words that finish each sentence.

1. Today most _____ people in Canada live in Quebec.
   Mexican   French   Palestinian

2. Smoke, dirt, and chemicals from factories and cars cause _____ .
   terrorism   PNTR   pollution

3. Americans can help save _____ by recycling.
   soldiers   technology   natural resources

4. After the Persian Gulf War, _____ became a free country again.
   Kuwait   East Germany   Iraq

5. _____ was part of the Soviet Union.
   Jordan   Israel   Russia

Name _____

◄ TIME LINE REVIEW ►
AMERICA'S STORY: SINCE 1865

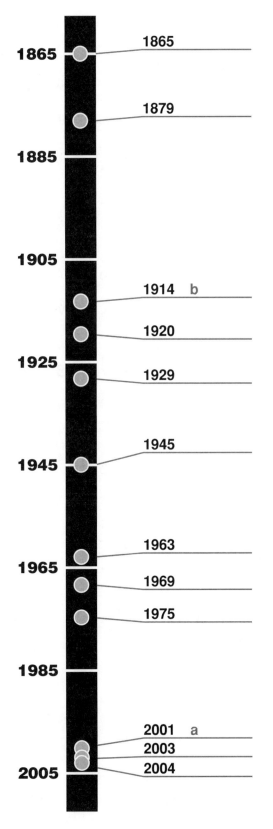

1865 — 1865

1879

1885

1905

1914   b

1920

1925 — 1929

1945 — 1945

1965 — 1963

1969

1975

1985

2001   a

2003

2004

2005

Read this time line from top to bottom. Put the letter of each sentence next to the correct date on the time line. The first two sentences are done for you.

a. The Patriot Act is passed by Congress.

b. World War I begins.

c. The Civil War ends and Reconstruction begins.

d. Women win the right to vote.

e. The United States drops two atomic bombs on Japan during World War II.

f. The Great Depression begins.

g. The Department of Homeland Security is created.

h. Martin Luther King, Jr., leads the March on Washington, D.C.

i. North Vietnam wins control of South Vietnam.

j. Americans walk on the moon.

k. George W. Bush is re-elected President of the United States.

l. Thomas Edison invents the electric light bulb.

Name _____

◖ FINAL TEST ◗

AMERICA'S STORY: SINCE 1865

True or False   Write **T** next to each sentence that is true. Write **F** next to each sentence that is false.

_____ 1. During the Cold War, Americans feared the spread of communism.

_____ 2. Jane Addams started Hull House in Chicago to help poor immigrants.

_____ 3. The Wright brothers flew the first airplane at Kitty Hawk, North Carolina.

_____ 4. General Eisenhower and the Allied soldiers invaded France during World War II.

_____ 5. César Chávez was one of the first Americans to walk on the moon.

_____ 6. The Internet allows millions of computers to communicate with one another.

Match Up   Finish each sentence in Group A with words from Group B. Write the letter of the correct answer on the blank line.

Group A

1. The _____ gave settlers free land on the Great Plains.

2. Martin Luther King, Jr., led a bus boycott in _____ .

3. The _____ put people back to work during the Great Depression.

4. _____ wrote newspaper stories about the problems immigrants had in America.

5. The United States helped Kuwait become free from Iraq during the _____ .

Group B

a. Montgomery, Alabama

b. Jacob Riis

c. New Deal

d. Homestead Act

e. Persian Gulf War

Name _____

◀ FINAL TEST ▶

AMERICA'S STORY: SINCE 1865

Sequencing Events Write the numbers **1**, **2**, **3**, **4**, and **5** next to these sentences to show the correct order.

_____ Congress added three amendments to the Constitution to help African Americans after the Civil War.

_____ *Apollo 11* landed on the moon in 1969.

_____ The United States attacked Iraq.

_____ In 1886 Samuel Gompers helped start a labor union called the American Federation of Labor.

_____ Japan attacked American ships at Pearl Harbor in 1941.

Finish the Sentence Draw a circle around the word or words that finish each sentence.

1. The idea that one country should rule other countries or colonies is _____ .
   democracy   appeasement   imperialism

2. The years after the Civil War when the southern states rejoined the United States was called _____ .
   Reconstruction   the Great Depression   the 1950s

3. _____ attacked American ships during World War I.
   Great Britain   France   Germany

4. The Nineteenth Amendment gave women the right to _____ .
   vote   study   own property

5. W.E.B. Du Bois helped start the _____ .
   PNTR   United Farm Workers   NAACP

6. Many Americans protested _____ .
   World War II   the Vietnam War   the Persian Gulf War

Name _____

◀ PRE-READING GUIDE ▶

1. What is the title of the chapter?

   _____

2. What do you already know about this period?

   _____

   _____

3. Read the questions in the "Find Out" box. What do you think you will learn from this chapter?

   _____

   _____

4. List two vocabulary words from the group of New Words. Write a definition from the Glossary next to each of your words.

   _____   _____

   _____   _____

5. Look at all the pictures in the chapter. List two things you think you will learn by reading the chapter.

   _____

   _____

6. Write three questions that you have about this topic. After you read the chapter, try to answer your questions.

   _____

   _____

   _____

Name _____

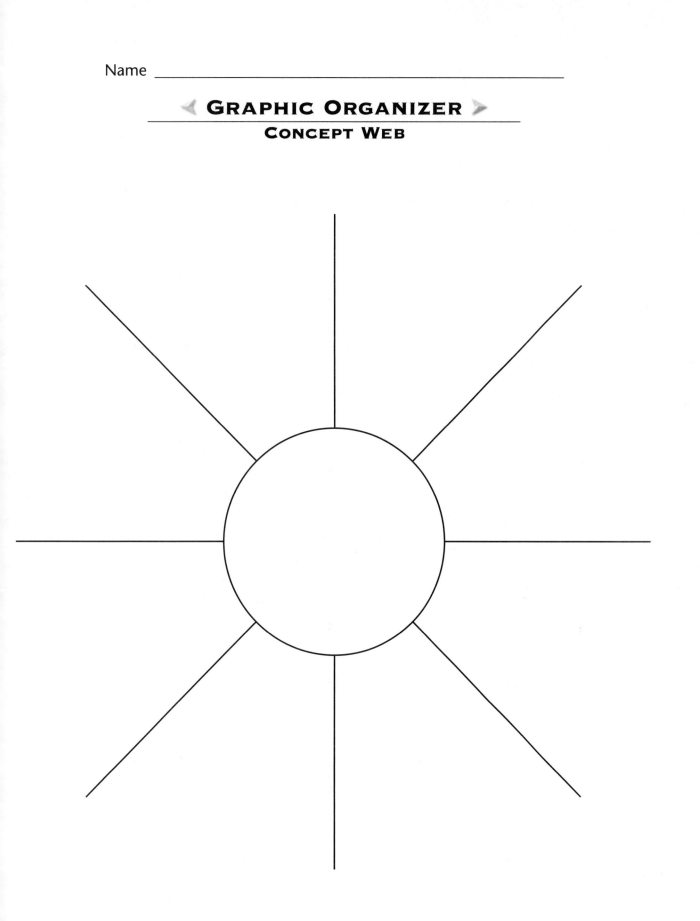

GRAPHIC ORGANIZER

CONCEPT WEB

Name _____

◄ GRAPHIC ORGANIZER ►
SEQUENCING

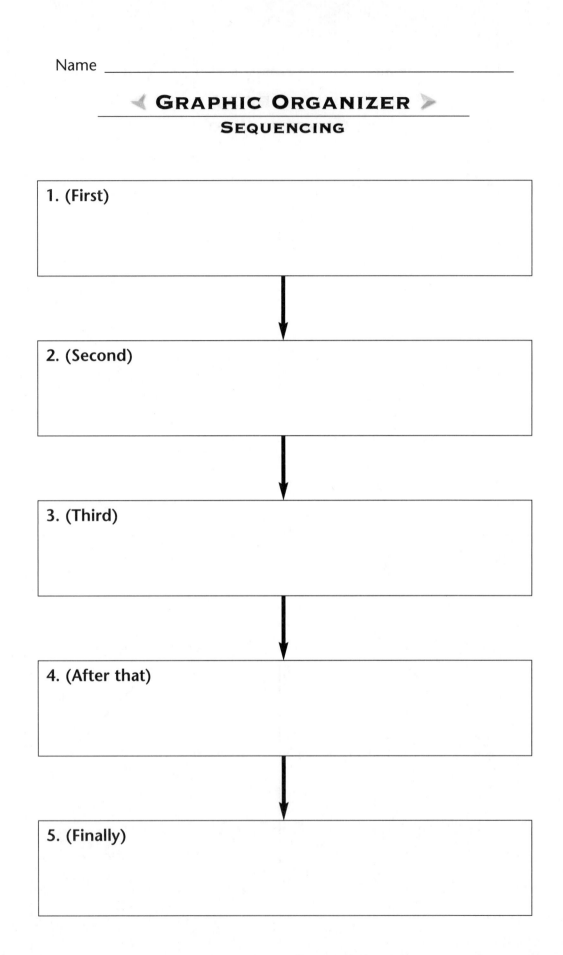

1. (First)

2. (Second)

3. (Third)

4. (After that)

5. (Finally)

Name _____

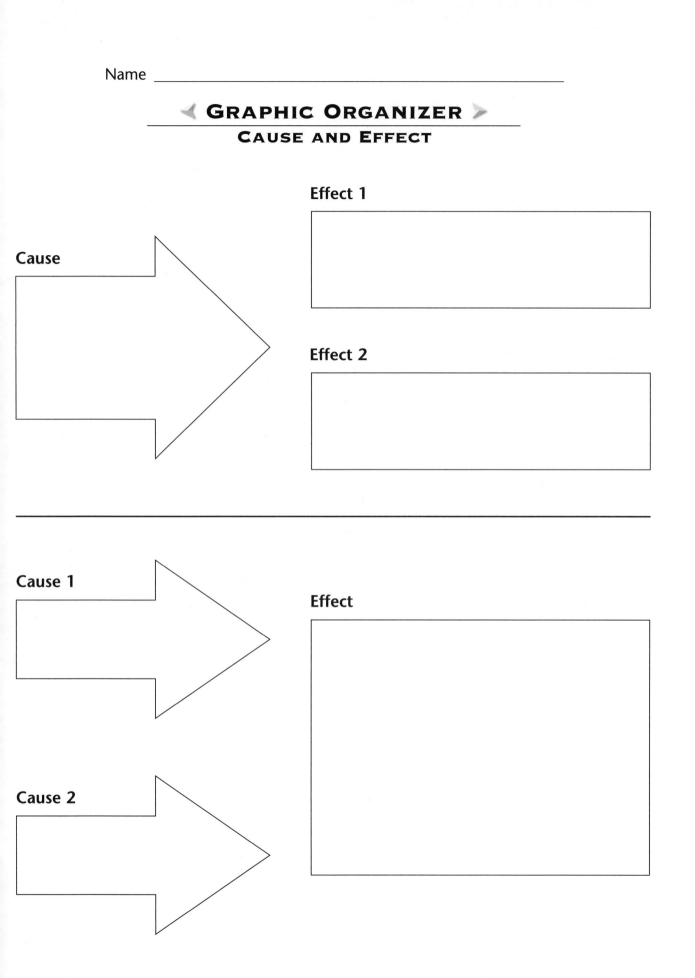

Effect 1

Cause

Effect 2

Cause 1

Effect

Cause 2

Name _____

◀ GRAPHIC ORGANIZER ▶
CAUSE AND EFFECT

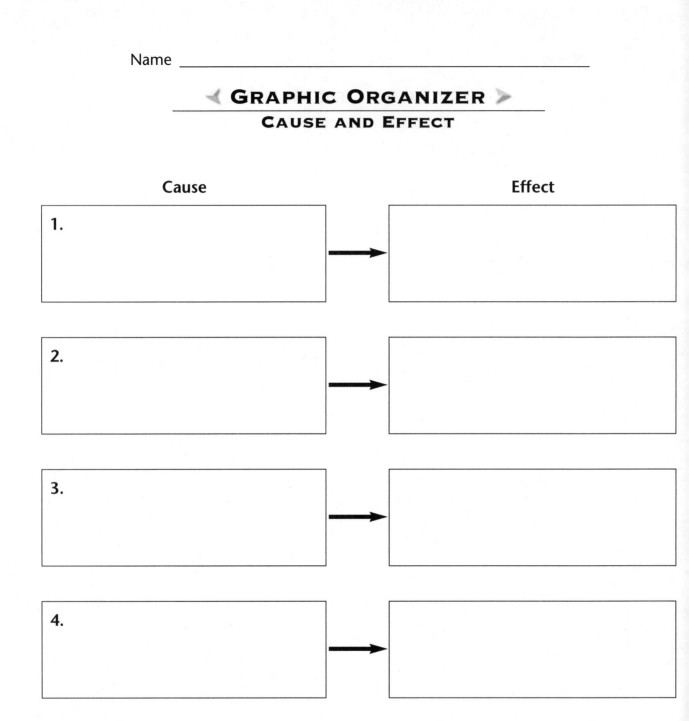

Cause   Effect

1.

2.

3.

4.

Name _____

◄ GRAPHIC ORGANIZER ►
FEATURE CHART

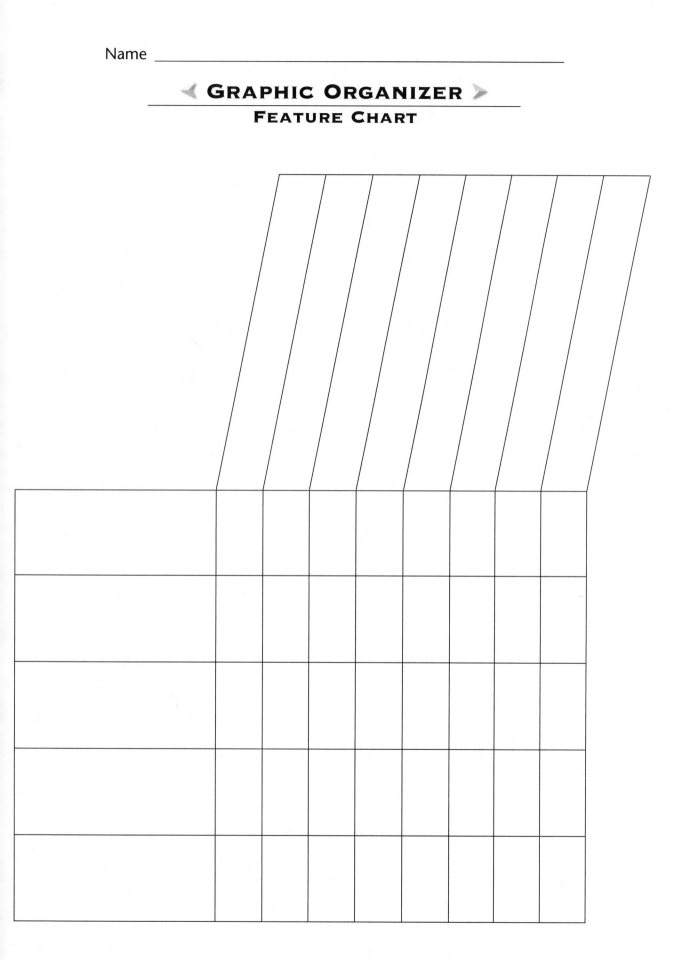

Name _____

◄ GRAPHIC ORGANIZER ►
EVENT DESCRIPTION

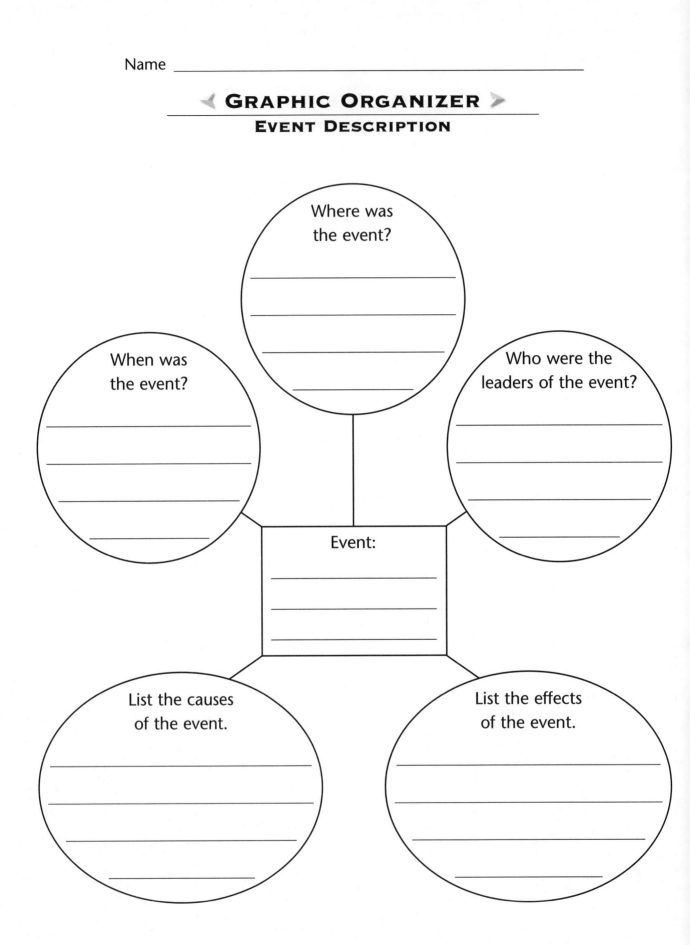

Where was
the event?

_____
_____
_____
_____

When was
the event?

_____
_____
_____
_____

Who were the
leaders of the event?

_____
_____
_____
_____

Event:

_____
_____
_____

List the causes
of the event.

_____
_____
_____
_____

List the effects
of the event.

_____
_____
_____
_____

Name _____

◀ GRAPHIC ORGANIZER ▶
MAIN IDEA AND SUPPORTING DETAILS

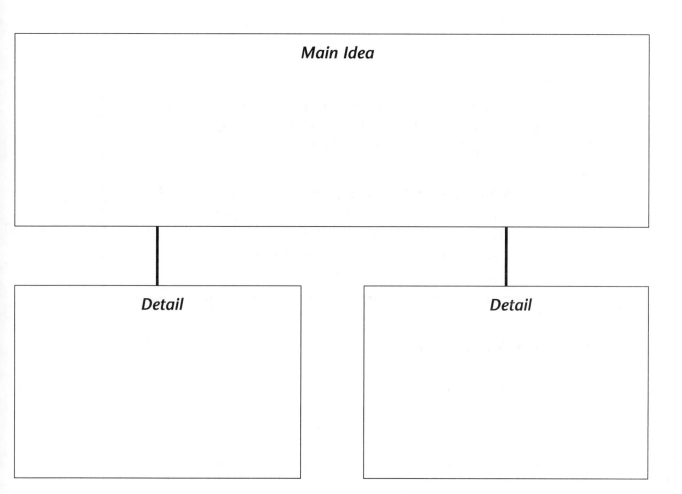

Name _____

Place tells what makes an area different from other areas in the world. Place tells about an area's land, plants, and weather, or **physical features**. It also tells about an area's people and what they built there, or **human features**.

The example below tells about Santa Fe, New Mexico. Follow the example to answer questions 1–2.

Example:

What are some physical features of Santa Fe?
Santa Fe is in high hills near the Sangre de Cristo Mountains. The Santa Fe River runs through Santa Fe.

What are some human features of Santa Fe?
Many Pueblo Indians live in villages around Santa Fe. The Spanish built the San Miguel Mission in Santa Fe. The city has many buildings made from bricks of dried mud. Santa Fe is the capital of New Mexico.

Describe the following place: _____

1. What are some physical features of this place? _____

   _____

   _____

   _____

2. What are some human features of this place? _____

   _____

   _____

   _____

Name _____

LOCATION

Location tells where a place is found. People use directions to tell the location of a place. People also say what a place is near and what is around it.

The example below tells the location of Washington, D.C. Follow the example to answer questions 1–2.

Example:

What is the location of Washington, D.C., using directions?
Washington, D.C., is in the eastern part of the United States. It is south of Maryland and north of Virginia.

What is near and around Washington, D.C.?
Washington, D.C., is on land between Maryland and Virginia. It is on the Potomac River. Washington, D.C., is near the Atlantic Ocean and the Chesapeake Bay.

Describe the location of the following place: _____

1. What are three ways you can tell the location of this place using directions?

_____

_____

_____

2. What is near and around the place? _____

_____

_____

_____

Name _____

◄ GEOGRAPHY THEME ►
MOVEMENT

Movement tells how people, goods, and ideas move from one place to another.

The example below tells about the movement to Indian Territory. Follow the example to answer questions 1–3.

Example:

Who or what was moved to Indian Territory?
The Native Americans of the Southeast, some of their belongings, and their ideas moved to the Indian Territory.

How did the Native Americans, their goods, and their ideas move to Indian Territory?
They took land routes and water routes. They walked, rode on horses, or traveled in boats. The Native Americans brought their languages, religions, and customs to the Indian Territory. They taught old stories and songs to their children.

Why did the American Indians move to Indian Territory?
The United States Army forced them to move because many Americans wanted to own the land in the Southeast.

Describe the following movement: _____

1. Who or what was moved—people, goods, and/or ideas? _____

   _____

2. How did the people, goods, and/or ideas move from one place to another?

   _____

   _____

3. Why did this movement happen? _____

   _____

   _____

Name _____

◄ GEOGRAPHY THEME ►
HUMAN/ENVIRONMENT INTERACTION

Human/Environment Interaction tells how people live in an area. It tells how people change an area or use the land to help them live and work.

The example below tells about the human/environment interaction during California's gold rush. Follow the example to answer questions 1–3.

Example:

How did people live in California during the gold rush?
They started up mining camps.

How did the miners change California?
They removed gold from rivers. They dug deep into the earth and mountains to remove gold. They dumped dirt and rocks into rivers. Most fish died in these dirty rivers. The rivers spread rocks over farmland, so less food was grown.

How did the environment change the miners' lives?
They spent their days mining. They slept at night in tents on cold ground. They had less food to eat because they killed the fish and could not grow food on the rocky farmland. Many miners got sick because they did not eat or sleep well.

Describe the following human/environment interaction: _____

1. How did people live in the area? _____

   _____

2. What are two ways the people changed the area? _____

   _____

   _____

3. What are two ways the environment changed the people? _____

   _____

   _____

Name _____

Region tells how places in an area are alike. Places in a region might have the same weather or kind of land. People in a region might share customs, ideas, and ways of life.

The example below tells about the region known as the South in 1861. Follow the example to answer questions 1–2.

Example:

What physical features did places in the South have that were alike?

The South had good soil. It also had rain and a warm climate during most of the year.

What human features did places in the South have that were alike?

The people in the South were mostly farmers. They grew cotton and other crops on farms and plantations. Slaves did most of the farm work on plantations. Southerners thought the South needed slavery and would fight to keep it.

Describe the following region: _____

1. What are three physical features that are alike in the region? _____

_____

_____

_____

2. What are three human features that are alike in the region? _____

_____

_____

_____

Name _____

◄ THE WRITING PROCESS ►

Step 1: Find ideas. Get ready to write.
Check all the ways you will get ready to write.

_____ list ideas

_____ read a library book

_____ talk about a topic in class

_____ use a concept web

Step 2: Write your paragraph or report.
Write your ideas using good sentences.

Step 3: Improve your writing.
Check all the ways you will correct and improve your writing.

_____ add missing facts

_____ improve the vocabulary

_____ check spelling

_____ sequence events correctly

_____ use capitals and periods correctly

_____ reread and correct your work

Step 4: Rewrite your work.
Check the way or ways you will rewrite your work.

_____ type it using a computer

_____ rewrite it with a pen by hand

Step 5: Share your writing.
Check all the ways you will share and save your writing.

_____ read it to the class

_____ hang it on a bulletin board

_____ publish it in a class magazine

_____ save it in a writing folder

Name _____

◄ RESEARCH ON THE WEB ►

The **World Wide Web** is a system of computers and computer files that are connected all over the world. Places that have information on the Web are called **websites**. You can use the Web to research many social studies topics.

Step 1: Choose one of the following topics to research on the Web:

Jamestown, Virginia	Harriet Tubman	Holocaust
Dolley Madison	Thomas Edison	César Chávez
Sequoya	muckrakers	Persian Gulf War

My topic is _____ .

Step 2: Turn on your computer, and log on to the Web. Choose one of these search engines to find websites about your topic. Search engines are tools that let you search for websites with the information you want.

www.onekey.com   www.yahooligans.com
www.ajkids.com   www.factmonster.com

My search engine is _____ .

Step 3: Type in the address for your search engine. Press the Enter key. Type your topic in the search box. Press the Enter key. List the names of two websites that your search engine found about your topic.

1. _____   2. _____

Step 4: Use your mouse to click the first website from Step 3. Read a few pages on this website. Write two facts you learned about your topic on the lines below. Then, go to the second website and list two different facts you learned.

Website #1	**Website #2**
Fact #1 _____	Fact #1 _____
_____	_____
Fact #2 _____	Fact #2 _____
_____	_____

Name _____

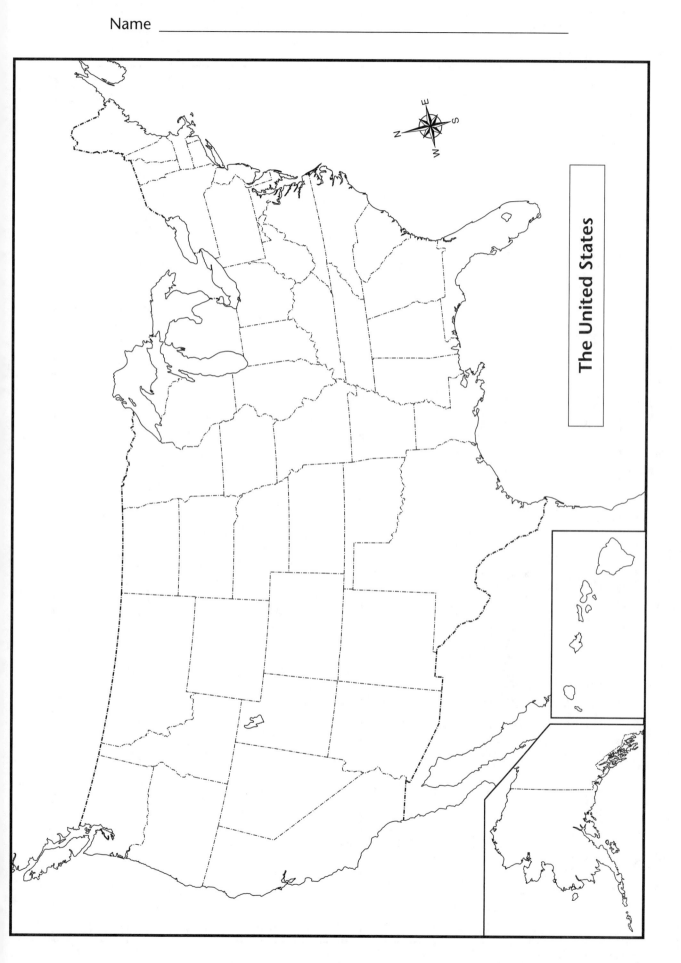

The United States

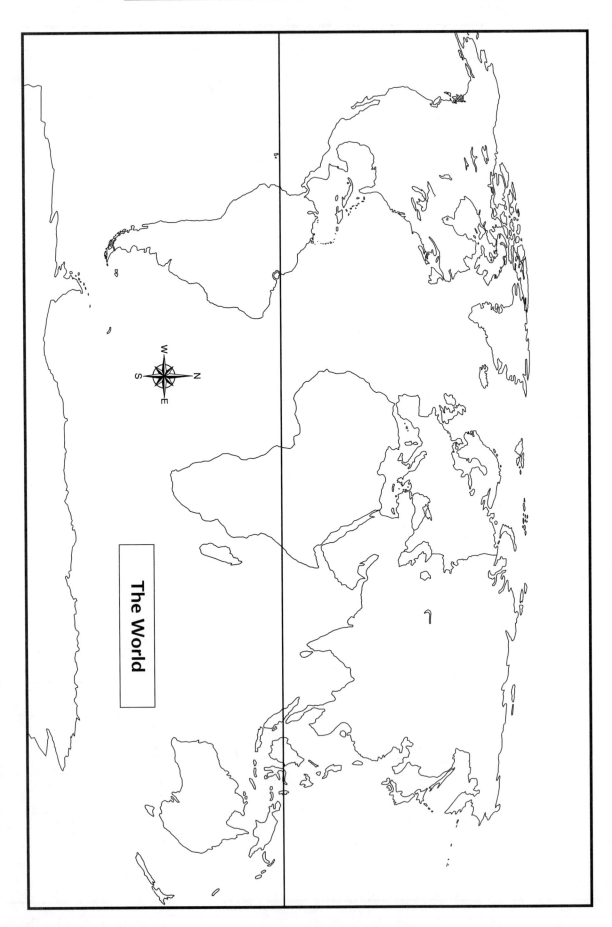

The World

124